FORGIVING
THE
NIGHTMARE

FORGIVING THE NIGHTMARE

MARK SOWERSBY

Paperback: 978-1-951475-18-5
eBook: 978-1-951475-19-2

Library of Congress Control Number: 2021920428

Arrow Press Publishing
245 Pemberly Blvd
Summerville, SC 29486

www.arrowpresspublishing.com

I dedicate this book to my wife and children. My hope is to leave you a legacy of forgiveness and a confidence in God's Word, love and grace. Let God be your strength.

Ephesians 6:10-18

CONTENTS

INTRODUCTION

It has been said that God has a sense of humor. Just look at the platypus — an egg laying, fur covered mammal with a duck's bill. I find it funny that God would ask me, a dyslexic special ed student who graduated high school with a third-grade reading level, to write a book. But the joke would be on me, because the Lord opened the door, made a way, and reminded me:

> *I can do all things through Christ Jesus who strengthens me.*
>
> *- Philippians 4:13 NIV*

Writing my testimony has been a calling and a journey of faith and obedience to the Lord.

When I started writing this book, I was asked a great question. "Who is your audience? Who are you writing the book to?" As my mind raced for an answer, the person who posed the question simply said, "You are writing the book to yourself." It clarified that I am writing to those who have walked through similar hurts, pains, rejection, and sorrows. I am writing to the ones who feel as powerless and lost as I felt.

The kind of book I looked for when I was discouraged, insecure, and afraid, was one that was short, to the point, genuine, and true. The thought of trying to struggle through reading a large book was intimidating. I feared it would reinforce my weaknesses and leave me feeling even more rejected. As I put pen to paper, I desired to write the kind of book that would not be overwhelming.

In this book, I have held to the ABC principles of sharing a Testimony. I spoke it audibly so that my testimony can be clearly heard, brief, to the point, and Christ-centered, giving God the glory. My hope is that as you read, you will find support, encouragement, and grace as you find the strength to forgive your nightmare. I trust the Scriptures will enlighten you, the stories will inspire you, and the prayers will strengthen you. Read it on its own or as a devotion with your Bible. Ponder it in your prayer closet or read it with a cup of coffee. However, you choose to read it, may the Lord be glorified.

As Paul said in 1 Corinthians 11:23, "What I received from the Lord I also pass on to you." Forgiving the Nightmare is my testimony. I wanted to write only that, nothing more and nothing less. I sought the Lord with much prayer, for His help to be vulnerable but not weak, honest but not sensational, confident yet not boastful.

Regardless of what your nightmare is, you are not alone. We all carry hurts and regrets and have nightmares which can hold us down, hold us back, and lie to us. I empathize with you. I understand. But I am also here to remind you, God loves you! Know this. Believe it and let it wash over you. You are loved!

*These three remain: faith, hope and love. But the greatest
of these is love.*

1 Corinthians 13:13 NIV

I offer you my testimony and story as a relay runner hands off a
baton. My hope and prayer is that my journey of forgiving the
nightmare will encourage, strengthen, and guide you to seek, strive,
and surrender to the Lord. May it help you to forgive others as
Christ has forgiven you. The journey of forgiveness is one we walk
every day, but we are not alone.

May the Lord give you friends, family, and a church to walk beside
you. An African Proverb says, "If you want to go fast, go alone. If
you want to go far, go together." The people who come beside you
on your journey are there for your successes and your failures.
They celebrate when you succeed, and they pick you up when you
fall. They humble you and honor you in ways only your friends and
family can.

The journey will not be easy as you tear down walls and build up
altars, but take heart, it is a worthwhile journey. I have been there. I
have wrestled with the past, battled through pain, and found solace
in prayer. I am a real person who is continually learning to trust the
Lord, day by day. I may not have all the answers, but I know the
One who does, and He is the one I want you to find through this
book.

The Lord helped me forgive my nightmare, and the Lord can help
you forgive your nightmare too.

*Then Peter opened his mouth, and said,
Of a truth I perceive that God is no respecter of persons:*
- Acts 10:34 KJV

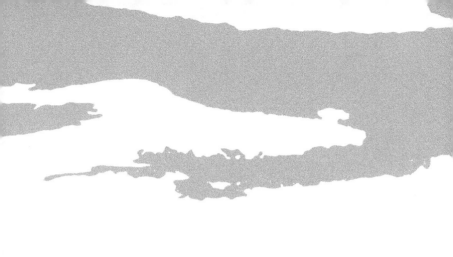

PART ONE
| MY STORY |

THE BEGINNING OF MY NIGHTMARE

MY MOM

Every story begins connected to someone else's story, and my story begins with my mom.

My mom was born in 1940, at the dawn of World War II. She was the only daughter born to my grandparents. Theirs was a blue-collar home where love was expressed by what people did, not so much by what people said. Religion was for Sundays, and Saturdays were for fun.

My grandparents had an arranged marriage. Not the kind you would find in the Gilded Age or Victorian Period, but nevertheless, still arranged. My grandfather was head over heels in love with my grandmother, even after their divorce in the mid-1940s. The rumor was, even though Grandpa got remarried a few times, he only loved one woman, my grandma.

My mother grew up in a home where she was spoiled with love. My grandfather referred to my mom as the apple of his eye every-

7

where he went, both in public and in private, until his death. My mom was in her mid-thirties when he passed away.

As you can imagine, my mom adored her dad. He took care of her completely. He did her shopping, made sure her car repairs were done, and even helped her pay her bills and organize her life. In hindsight though, his love looked more like enabling. Years later my mom confessed, as much as she loved her dad, his love did not prepare her for life.

My mom's dreams were not to be rich and famous, an actress or a dancer. My mom's dreams were to be what many women of her generation dreamed to be, a wife and a mother. It was a vocation she hoped for, longed for, and prayed for. She met her handsome Prince Charming in high school. He promised her the world, love, and respect. Mom graduated in 1958, married him in 1959, and gave birth to my older brother in 1960. The dream she always wanted was the fairy tale she was living.

Yet, life was not all it seemed. Like many families of that era, you kept your problems at home behind closed doors. You painted a smile on your face and hid your pain behind a veil of secrecy. From the outside looking in, everything looked great. But things were not great. Her husband, that high school sweetheart, would be cruel and abusive with his words and his actions. Even though another child would be born, the fairy tale world my mother had longed for was slowly breaking apart. Her husband found comfort in other women and insulted his wife, my mother. He stole her beauty, importance, and value. For the rest of my mom's life, she would carry insecurities, fears, and hurts. She saw life through a broken lens. When her dream died, her hope died also. The lines on her face and the hurt in her eyes were constantly before us.

She moved back home to her mother who took in her and her children. Her father again did everything for her. She felt like a failure, someone who had lost their significance. Needing to provide for her family, she found a factory job. Still young and looking for love and acceptance, my father entered her life promising comfort, friendship, and love. He made her laugh and feel pretty. She would say, "Markie, your dad and I were just best friends." My mom never held the same depth of anger at my dad as she did with her first husband; even though my dad broke her heart, when he confessed, he was married to another, and left her with a child.

> *For you created my inmost being; you knit me together in my mother's womb.*
>
> *- Psalm 139:13 NIV*

Once again, she was filled with more pain, more regrets, and more insecurities. Time went on. In my early years, I remember being with my mom as we watched Sesame Street, Mr. Rogers, and even the old television show, To Tell the Truth.

We lived with my grandma. I remember her heart was big and her voice was soft. I only knew her in the winter of her life; she was sickly, bed ridden, and her husbands were both gone. My mom was not only her daughter, but also her caretaker and nurse. She was grateful to be able to help her mom, but she also felt burdened by the demands that were relegated to her. During the time we lived with grandma, I did kid stuff; built forts, rode my bike, and played with my friends. It was the 1970s. My brother and sister were teenagers. My mother's pains gripped her deeply through the years. I did not know it then, but as I look back, I see it now. She became a shut in; she was angry, fearful, and sad at the same time.

Around 1977, shortly after my grandmother passed away, a man came into our home. He was twenty years my mom's younger. Like a stray dog, my mom took him in. She said she loved him. She felt broken because of her hurts and regrets, and with him there were no expectations. He was even more broken than she was. It was not love, it was a toxic mixture of dysfunctions, where both found something in their hurts from the other. Like every other man in my mother's life, he too would become an abuser, a liar, and a thief. The abuse was not only aimed at my mom. This time it focused on me. The nightmare consumed my life for seven years.

MY NIGHTMARE

I can't remember the exact day, but I do remember the cracking sound of the threshold, the smell of the attacker's breath and sweat, the touch, the lies, and the confusion that came to me the first time I was raped. Lost is the only word I can find to express what I was thinking. I was only seven years old, just a child. I clearly remember the throbbing and bleeding from the sexual abuse that just occurred, and my mother's husband saying, "Markie, don't tell anyone because they will take you away from your mom." From that day forth, I was a victim, an object of pleasure to be abused.

I was abused for the next seven years of my life. I was raped almost daily, often a few times a day. Not only was my mother's husband raping me, but I was sold to other men. I was frequently forced into an old van and told to stay; my mother's husband would leave, and the sliding door would slam shut. A few minutes later the door would open, and I would become the object of someone else's perverted fantasy.

I was cut just so someone could watch me bleed, stabbed just in case I thought of fleeing, drugged just to amuse the attacker, and raped constantly. I tried, as a child, to make sense of all this; maybe it was not real, maybe I was not real. Where was my real dad? Where was my defender? Where was my mom? I died more each day; I was just a shell. I was broken and brainwashed; this was my life, my lot, and I believed it was my fault.

What was happening in the dark was affecting the whole family. The atmosphere at home was oppressive and as my brother moved out, my sister was not far behind. My mom ran to her new husband, my abuser, fearing she would be alone. My grandma had passed away. I felt abandoned and cast away; that other people were more important than I was.

After some time, I built up the courage to tell my mom what was happening. I knew it would stop. My mom would help me. Everything would end after I told her. The afternoon I told my mom all that was happening, she looked at me and told me she loved me. She called her husband into the room and made him promise he would never do "it" again. Then she said, "Markie, don't tell anyone, this is a family secret." The need for privacy and the familiarity of secrecy, of keeping your problems at home behind closed doors would always be in my mom, until her passing.

The next morning, my mother's husband entered my room, but this time he pretended he was in a trance, an unconscious state. Whatever innocence I still had left, died that day. I remember shaking him, begging, and crying out, "BUT YOU PROMISED! YOU PROMISED, YOU WOULD NOT DO THIS ANYMORE!" Yet, he kept up the charade, and acted as one possessed. Out of the many attacks I had to endure, this one demoralized me more profoundly than any of the previous ones. Then my abuser roused himself from his sham and gave me one of the most intense beatings I ever got from him. His perversion had been exposed, and the fear of getting caught escalated his brutality and intensified his rage more than ever. Today, my front tooth is a replacement, a result of the baseball bat with which he used to beat me. My life continued, abused at home and bullied at school, with no father and a mother lost in hurt...

> *But you, God, see the trouble of the afflicted;*
> *you consider their grief and take it in hand.*
> *The victims commit themselves to you;*
> *you are the helper of the fatherless.*
>
> *- Psalm 10:14 NIV*

Our home was filled with drugs, alcohol, abuse, and pain. My mother's husband was a drug dealer. Not like those you see on TV, he was much dirtier and sleazier. I remember one day, though I don't know how, the state got involved, and that night at the table, my mom again begged me not to tell anyone our family secrets.

At fourteen two important things happened:

First, I fought back! By this time, I think my attacker believed I was so broken and conditioned to the abuse that I would never fight back. The routine of daily perversion and sick dysfunction was as constant as the sun rising and setting. The place where he took me that day was an empty, cold, dirty apartment with a shaggy green carpet that smelled of stale cigarettes. It was a place of despair. The abuse started in the usual way: with threats, lies, and commands. This time though, something rose within me. With all my might, I pushed him away. I kicked my feet and swung my fists. I pulled my clothes back up and ran as fast and as hard as I could from that place.

Second, I found my defender. One day, while playing with my cousins, we found ourselves hiding under a canoe that had been leaned against a fence. We were talking, and I started to tell my cousins all that was happening to me. I shared with them the details and the experiences of what was taking place. They encouraged me to tell their dad, my uncle. He became my defender.

I remember very clearly my uncle asking me directly, "Markie, is this true?" I said "Yes, it is." He believed me. He stood up for me. He protected me. My aunt came into the room and held me tight. My mother's husband was supposed to pick me up that afternoon. When he got there, my normally gentle uncle erupted in my defense. I did not go home with my abuser that day. My uncle informed me I would be staying with him for a while. Mom would simply say it was good I stayed with them, never acknowledging the real reason. I ended up living with my uncle and aunt for over a year. When I eventually returned home, I was never raped or attacked again. My uncle was my mother's younger brother. His children and I were close in age, and in those days, he was the closest person I had to a father figure. Unfortunately, we lost my uncle to cancer when I was a senior in high school.

SALVATION AND MY FAITH

SALVATION

The summer of my sixteenth birthday, I was back living with my mom and her husband. I was older, bigger, and stronger, and determined never to be sexually abused again. Even though I was never physically abused again, abusers still abuse, and there was still death in his words and poison in his mouth. I was living at home, but I never wanted to be at home. I was that kid that stayed with my friends for dinner. I deliberately stayed too late, and then slept over because I wanted to be anywhere other than home.

That year I learned the power of being a victim. I discovered the control that guilt gave me. I found that my family gave me everything I wanted. I won every argument. I was never corrected. My mother's guilt and shame grew and with my immaturity and anger it became an unhealthy mix. Years later I dealt with it at an altar with the Lord, where I learned not to be a victim but to be victorious in Jesus.

Eventually many of my friends started to explore, experiment, and test authority by smoking pot, drinking alcohol, and doing other rebellious things. I knew where that road would lead me, and I did not want to go there. I did not rebel in the typical teenage way. My rebellion drove me to want to make money, earn credit, and be responsible. I needed to be completely different from the home I lived in. I genuinely believe my attacker wanted me to be broken and destroyed, but God had a different plan and restoration was His ambition.

I was far from perfect. I did not want drugs or alcohol, but girls were another story. I was a messed-up teenager, not knowing what it meant to be in a healthy relationship. I felt I needed a girlfriend to complete me, heal me, and make me whole.

We lived in an apartment complex with a pool. I spent as much time as I could at that pool. There was a particular lifeguard, who all the teenage boys were smitten with because of her kindness and beauty. She talked to me and was nice to me. One day she asked me if I wanted to go to church. I did not know a lot about church, but I didn't care. I just wanted to go with her! I ran home and got changed. She picked me up, then introduced me to her boyfriend.

That day, I went to a church unlike any I had ever been to before. My family believed in God, but we didn't go regularly to church. Church was the big building where we went, maybe on Christmas. This church was different. The hall was full of young people, the pastor was only a few years older than me, and his hair was long! The lights went low. They played guitars and drums. Then people started singing, but not songs not from a hymnal. They raised their hands to worship, and I stood there like a statue, in shock at all of I was experiencing. The people were nice, but I was a bit uncomfortable. People wanted to hug me, but as you can imagine, I was not a huge fan of hugging. They told me God loved me, and God wanted me to love Him. I thought to myself, "They are nice, but this is not my thing."

I soon noticed the youth pastor and his wife lived in the same apartment complex as I did. The pastor's wife had recently had a baby, and she frequently walked around the apartment complex pushing her stroller. Occasionally she would see me, say hello, and invite me back to the church youth group.

One of the last days of that summer, just after I turned sixteen, I went back to that interesting church with the dim lights where they played guitars and drums. The youth group sang their songs, and the pastor explained who God is. The words he spoke penetrated my heart. At the end of the meeting as everyone began leaving and the youth scattered, it started raining and I needed a ride home. One of the kids in the youth group offered to give me a ride. He was a bit older than I and already had his driver's license and a car. When I got in, he asked me what I thought about the pastor's message. We talked about it, then he asked me a question that would change my life forever. He asked me if I wanted to ask the Lord Jesus into my heart to be my Lord and Savior. Without hesitation, though also not fully understanding, I said "Yes", and we prayed together. I prayed a prayer that I would come to know as the sinner's prayer.

> ...*if you confess with your mouth the Lord Jesus*
> *and believe in your heart that God has raised Him from*
> *the dead, you will be saved.*
>   - *Romans 10:9 NIV*

The next day I woke up to the sounds of cars honking their horns in the parking lot. I'll never forget my mom looking out the window yelling, "What the *#&@$!" There was the youth pastor yelling, "Mark!" with a parking lot full of youth from the night before. They were all inviting me, waiting for me, and expecting me to go with them. I ran out of the house and went on my first youth-group trip.

We climbed Mount Monadnock where I met a lot of other young people. I felt normal, I felt accepted, I felt appreciated. Quickly that youth group and church became the center of my life. I spent all my time getting involved, volunteering, and building friendships. I was challenged, accepted, and I was loved. I experienced correction with love and faced challenges with hope. I found faith, friends, and sanctuary. If the door was open, I was there.

Robert Frost authored a poem called, The Road Not Taken. Part of the poem really spoke to me,

> *Two roads diverged in a wood, and I—*
> *I took the one less traveled by,*
> *And that has made all the difference.*

In many ways, I believe this is how victims feel. The path of the neglected, mistreated, and abused is often determined by the decisions made at significant moral and spiritual crossroads. We stand at these crossroads and question, "Why me? Why did this happen? Where were you God? Why should I trust You? Where is my justice? How do I know You will be there the next time I'm hurt? Why do you want me? Why didn't you protect me? What do I have left to give? Why should I choose to walk down the path less traveled?"

While in prayer, God spoke to me, not in anger or frustration, but with such love and kindness, my spirit and heart had never heard before. He awakened within me hope, love, peace, and grace. His words were foreign and beyond anything my life, heart, understanding, and my mind could comprehend. He spoke to me in His Word and said, "I have given you more than you promised me, more than you could ever dream of." He said to me, "I will always be with you." He spoke to me in the still small voice in the way only He can. He awakened inside me a passion for Him that was greater than the hurts of my past. He took me from a life of just survival to a life where I could thrive in Him. And that has made all the difference.

I started to believe in something I could not see, I started to hold onto something that was bigger than me. For the first time, His love became greater than my past. His ways became bigger than my fears. His road was the one less traveled, but before I knew it, I began walking with Him down that road. I began singing His praises and proclaiming His name for I know I am His child, and He is my God.

Over the next ten years my life revolved around the church. I got plugged in and anchored to my faith. I grew up there, and like any place you grow up, you make your mistakes, and have some regrets, but you learn your lessons, and have your friends and loved ones to help you carry life's burdens.

THE CALL AND THE FIGHT

Not long after I said the sinner's prayer in my friend's car, I attended a youth convention service. By the end of the service, I was at the altar truly desiring God's will and direction for my life. I believe God's grace and mercy covered me as I poured out all of me in prayer that evening. The still small voice of the Lord spoke to me at that altar. It wasn't audible but it was in my heart, my mind, and my soul. I heard in my spirit, "I'm calling you to be a pastor, a shepherd, someone who will proclaim my name." I was in shock and disbelief and like Moses at the burning bush, I proceeded to tell God all the reasons why I could not be a pastor.

> For I know the plans I have for you," declares the Lord, "plans to prosper you and not to harm you, plans to give you hope and a future.
> - Jeremiah 29:11 NIV

One of the casualties of my childhood was my education. I have wrestled with dyslexia and learning disabilities from the beginning of school. I found no support or help within my abusive home. I was put in special education classes with an Individual Education Plan (IEP). I believe I was rushed through most of my classes. As a result, I graduated high school with a third grade reading ability. When I heard the voice of the Lord in my spirit, overwhelming fear and doubt rose within me. I knew I did not have the ability to go to Bible college. I could barely read or write. How could God use me?

Life went on. I got a job, and volunteered as a youth leader at church, never forgetting what the Lord said to me that day at the altar. Every time I put my head to my pillow, or was in my quiet place, I would hear the Lord calling me to step out, walk by faith and do what He told me to do. The longer I waited, the louder the doubts and fears became. How could I do what He said? I was messed up. I could hardly read. Education was a mountain I could not climb. But the echo of God's calling still rang in my spirit despite all my doubts and fears.

One night at a youth Christmas party one of the other leaders, a strong, godly woman, asked me to read the Christmas story from the book of Luke in front of the entire youth group. I tried to make excuses to get out of reading, I gave her all kinds of reasons why I couldn't read that night. But she was the kind of person that did not take no for an answer. My anxieties were high and my fears deep. I got up and I read... I read slowly... broken up... stumbling over my words, but the group was kind and showed me mercy and grace.

After the service, she let me know that she home schooled all her children and offered to tutor me in reading at their house. I was desperately in need of the help, so I agreed. I pictured that I would go over, and we would be in a private room as I learned to read. A place where I would have one on one tutoring without the embarrassment of an audience. That was not the case.

I sat at the kitchen table with her seven-year-old. As life in a busy home went on around us, we learned phonics and word structure. Together we learned how to read. Sometimes her seven-year-old would say "No, that is not the way you say..." It was tough, I was scared, embarrassed, and it was humbling to be corrected by a seven-year-old child, but God had made a way for me to step into my calling and I chose to follow His leading. Unbeknownst to me, her oldest daughter, Jennifer, began to fall in love... with me.

Years later, when I was thirty-three, my teacher's oldest daughter became my wife. He not only provided a way for me learn so I could step into my calling, He also provided me with the person who would be my helpmate, encourager, and best friend.

> *"For my thoughts are not your thoughts, neither are your ways my ways," declares the Lord. "As the heavens are higher than the earth, so are my ways higher than your ways and my thoughts than your thoughts."*
> *- Isaiah 55:8-9 NIV*

Although I became a stronger reader, the challenge of dyslexia caused me to be deathly afraid of education. I visited Christian colleges where I could study how to be a pastor. I'll never forget visiting the first school, sitting with the administrators. As they looked at my transcripts, I could see in their eyes and from the expressions on their faces that they were concerned with my lack of experience, accomplishments, and academics. Very kindly, they would direct me to go home, take some junior college courses. After completing them, they might reconsider me for their school. Visiting several schools and being told *no* in diverse ways confirmed my fears and emphasized my lack of confidence in my own abilities. I remember praying to God in my brokenness, "God, I tried but they don't want me." Again, I put the call on the back burner. I was not ready to submit to God and the call He put on my life. I kept running from my call, holding tight to my excuses.

In an effort to make myself feel better, I bought something I had always wanted. I bought a brand-new truck. I was the first of my family to go to a dealership and buy a new vehicle off the lot. My credit was strong, and my finances were good. One day, after only having the truck for a few months, I was driving and singing praises to the Lord. The Spirit of the Lord became so strong in the cab of the truck that I had to pull over. Tears were streaming down my face as God's voice spoke to my spirit, my heart, and my soul once again. "I've called you to go.", He said. He spoke strongly, compassionately, and authoritatively. The tears continued pouring down my face as I heard in my Spirit the words from Joshua:

> *"...Choose for yourself this day whom you will serve…."*
> *- Joshua 24:15 NIV*

I believe God was beckoning me, commanding me to yield to His will. I chose to believe and decided to step out in faith.

I grew up in the shadow of a Bible College, though I really knew nothing about it. They seemed a little different: they wore uniforms, boys sat on one side and girls on the other. I thought they were very legalistic. I remember saying to God, "I don't want to go there." Yet, my spirit again heard Him, and with authority God told me to go and talk with the school. I made an appointment with the Dean of Students. I "knew" they would reject me, like every other school had done. I was almost hoping they would, so I could say to God, "See I told you so."

> *Trust in the Lord with all your heart, and lean not on your*
> *own understanding; in all your ways acknowledge Him,*
> *and He shall direct your paths.*
>
> *- Proverbs 3:5-6 NKJV*

As I sat across the desk from the dean, I waited for him to reject me as every other school had. He looked at me, and asked, "Mark are you called by God?" I said, "Yes." He got up from his desk, walked over to a picture window, tapped to get the attention of a staff member who was walking by. He introduced me to her. The dean informed me that she had just arrived on campus a few days before. She came with a passion and call to begin a learning center for students who need a little bit more academic help. I enrolled that day and became the first student utilizing the learning center. I sold my new truck back to the dealer, freeing me to begin college. The academics were not easy. I had many challenges, but I also had help. Today, I'm a proud graduate of Zion Bible Institute, now known as Northpoint Bible College.

I got connected and immersed myself into college life. Zion Bible Institute had a program at that time which was put in place to help keep the cost of tuition down. It was called Students Participating in Campus Experience (SPICE). Each student was required to do volunteer work on campus each week. The school would assign you to a department, such as the kitchen, library, housekeeping, snow removal, etc. Students on a ministry, worship, or traveling team were required to volunteer fewer hours in the SPICE program.

The school held open auditions for the traveling ministry team, and I tried out. Walking into the audition room was intimidating. The room was filled with multi-generational pastor and missionary kids who grew up in the church and knew how to act on the platform. I felt like a fool, and in my mind, I was already defeated even before I opened my mouth. Why would anybody want me? The ministry team represented the school, and I knew I was the weakest student there. I was called up front and asked to ad-lib a scene. In that moment I realized I was good at acting, not because I had lessons, but because I had been acting my entire life. I had put on a smile and pretended everything was ok for so long, acting became second nature. I auditioned and was invited to join the traveling ministry team called the Sentinels. I was going to represent my school!

Joining this team had a profound impact on my life. It helped develop me as a preacher and taught me how to present the gospel of Jesus Christ to the world. The Lord used me powerfully one night in Canada. After I had shared my testimony before a crowd, we opened the altar and invited people to come forward for prayer. The team gathered in front of the platform, there were nine of us and I was standing in the center. I will never forget praying with the people. Some held me tight, while others wet my shirt with their tears. It was overwhelming, and it was a powerful night of prayer. At one point, I looked down the line and I couldn't see the end of it. So many people wanted to pray with me. Mothers, asking me if their children would forgive them like I forgave my mom, and victims, asking me if they could experience the same freedom I had.

I looked to the heavens and said, "Lord, who am I? What do I have? What can I say to people to help? There are so many hurts. Who am I to stand in such a place?" The Lord spoke to my heart and said, "You have a powerful testimony, and I will use it. You will write it down." I chuckled in my spirit. "Lord, me? I can barely write. If I write this down, what will I call it?" That night the Lord said, "You will call it Forgiving the Nightmare." The Lord very clearly placed in my heart the seed of the ministry and book you are reading now.

MY FAITH

The scars of my abuse, both physically and emotionally, were still with me. I knew the Scriptures and I trusted in the Lord, yet I still carried the pain, hurt, anger and fear. Even though the abuse was years behind me, I still felt like junk, insecure, and messed up. The victim chip on my shoulder was still big and loud. I often tell people that I was not raised, I survived my childhood.

I had my familiar excuses and hurts, I knew them well, and they knew me. I believed they protected me and justified my actions and deeds. One day while at a powerful church service, the kind where you can feel the tangible presence of the Lord, the Lord began to challenge me. At that altar my Heavenly Father convicted me with love, compassion, and tender authority.

> *My son, do not despise the Lord's discipline, and do not resent his rebuke, because the Lord disciplines those he loves, as a father, the son he delights in.*
> *- Proverbs 3:11-12 NIV*

The Lord and I wrestled as I struggled to let go of anger and unforgiveness. He dealt with how I saw myself and how I saw others, like my mother, my family, and my mother's husband. I will never forget that night at the altar, where He convicted me of my unforgiveness. He then taught me how to forgive and He led me to forgiveness. I was transformed from victim to victor. I remember telling the Lord, "If I am not a victim, who am I?" I felt the Lord say, "You are my child." That revelation washed over me daily.

I was still fearful, still running away from my past, my attacker, and myself. I wish I could tell you when I got up from the altar everything was fixed, but the journey was just beginning. The Lord's challenge to forgive and let go of the anger, to remember that I was no longer a victim, but His child, was constant in my heart from that moment on. Forgiveness, what is it? What does it look like? How do I know if I have truly forgiven? Sometimes, the process felt too raw. It was overwhelming and uncomfortable. When the familiar wounds rose, triggering anger, unhealthy feelings and insecurities that threatened to overwhelm me, each one was turned over to God until they no longer had a hold on me.

The lies, insecurities and anger were replaced as I clung to the knowledge that God was there. Always there. He was there through the darkest hours. His presence was constant.

The Lord was faithful, working that moment at the altar into the very fiber of my being until the insecurities and anger diminished as the grace and mercy of the Lord grew. The day came when I had forgiven. I let go of the anger and realized I was no longer a victim. I was His child. He made me victorious.

...he who began a good work in you will carry it on to completion until the day of Christ Jesus.

- Philippians 1:6b NIV

After college, I was off to the races to share the good news of the gospel, doing whatever I was asked to do, although excited to call myself "pastor." I remember the night I was ordained. For a moment, I felt the joy and the excitement of the call to pastor. That moment was quickly replaced with a deepening awareness of the responsibility of this call. I have served the Lord over the years as a children's pastor, junior-high pastor, visitation pastor, assistant pastor, and lead pastor.

Jennifer and I married in 2003. A couple years later we had a son. He was born with ten fingers and ten toes, a healthy baby boy. My heart was full. I was a proud daddy! At his birth, the doctor put him in my arms. It was amazing how much I was consumed with love, a sense of awe, and commitment, a willingness to sacrifice for him.

As I held my son with the passion of a new father, tears of joy filling my eyes, I held him close and prayed. Suddenly an alarming feeling swept over me as I realized that nobody had ever loved or sacrificed that much for me. The joy of being a father filled me, but the sorrow of feeling abandoned filled me too. Once again, my attacker's behavior was stealing the joy of the moment. I was upset with myself. Why was he still in my head, abusing me at this moment? Then the still, small voice of the Lord spoke again, and He reminded me that He always loved me. He is, and always was, my Abba Father, He is committed to me, and sacrificed all for me. The peace of the Lord came over me and my wife as we celebrated the birth of our first child together.

Today we have four children. Our son was followed by our three daughters whom I love. Of all the titles that I have, "Dad" is one of my favorites and the one that demands the most from me. Thinking of my children, I am reminded of the confidence each one of my children demonstrate. They are always willing to try new things, to go first, and they never hold back.

They are comfortable just being who they are.

I asked the Lord, "How come my children have so much confidence?" The Lord said to me, "because they have a father." I said, "I am not confident. I run away. I doubt myself and I am fearful." Then the Lord said to me. "When a child has a father who loves, provides, protects, guides, and prays for them, the child grows confident." Then I said, "but God, I did not have a father, how can I give what I don't have?" Then he said, "You have me, and I have always been your Heavenly Father."

The goodness of God is so sweet and faithful.

One of my mentors once shared that every wonderful thing that happened in his life, happened at an altar. The same is true for me. I was called at an altar, married at an altar, dedicated my children at an altar, and received healing at an altar.

An altar is a place of surrender, sacrifice, and remembrance. Throughout the Bible we see God's people building altars and laying their sacrifice upon it. By faith they believed God would accept their sacrifice, be pleased with it, that it would atone for their sins and draw them closer to God. Today we don't build altars of atoning for our sins because the greatest sacrifice was given to us when Jesus laid down His life on the altar of the cross and died for us.

The attitude of the altar still needs to be about us. While we don't offer burnt offerings anymore, I surrender my life, my will, and my heart to become a living sacrifice.

> *Therefore, I urge you, brothers and sisters, in view of God's mercy, to offer your bodies as a living sacrifice, holy and pleasing to God—this is your true and proper worship. Do not conform to the pattern of this world, but be transformed by the renewing of your mind. Then you will be able to test and approve what God's will is—his good, pleasing, and perfect will.*
>
> *-Romans 12:1-2 NIV*

Daily, I choose to surrender my selfish desires, imperfect life, and hard heart not to gain favor or acceptance, for I am loved and accepted by God, and I am saved by grace and receive it by faith. Paul told us to be living sacrifices. The altar becomes a place to reflect, recall, respond, repent, and resolve, my thoughts, attitudes, and actions. It is a place to renew my mind, heart, and relationship with the Lord.

Altars are a place of remembrance, in Joshua 3 and 4 we find the account of when the Israelites crossed the Jordan on dry ground. The Lord demonstrated to them that He is the living God. He had them gather 12 stones from the middle of the Jordan river to build an altar.

> *We will use these stones to build a memorial. In the future your children will ask you, 'What do these stones mean?' Then you can tell them, 'They remind us that the Jordan River stopped flowing when the Ark of the Lord's Covenant went across.' These stones will stand as a memorial among the people of Israel forever.*
>
> *- Joshua 4:6-7 NLT*

When God leads you through a difficult time, record it, so when the next difficult time comes you will be reminded what the Lord did. Psalm 136 is a chapter that recounts the goodness and faithfulness of God for the Israelites. Reflect on what God has done for you. Hebrews 11 provides examples of people who lived by faith and followed God before they received what was promised. Living a life of faith in God is a journey worth taking. Find something that will remind you of the goodness of God and put it on your altar where it will daily remind you to reflect, respond, repent, and resolve that which God is calling you to.

MY JOURNEY

MY JOURNEY

When I speak about forgiveness, I am often asked, "Did you really forgive your mom, your abuser, your family, and your past?" Yes. I forgave because Christ has forgiven me, and He calls us to forgive others. I was tired of being angry. The entire world told me I had the right to be angry, to be mad, and that I could cut my family off and never speak to them again. People would understand. It was OK. It was my "right." Unforgiveness was linking me to my abusers, connecting me to the hurts, pains, and poison of the abuse that ran so deep within me. Forgiving was, and still is, the only way to be set free.

Some People reach in to find themselves; others reach out to discover themselves. God calls us to reach up and die to ourselves. Dying to self only comes through praying, trusting, having faith, and being filled with God's love, the Holy Spirit, and the Word of God. Only then can the bonds of dysfunction, insecurities, and self-hatred be broken. Only In Christ, could I be set free from the chains that were still controlling so many areas of my life.

I wanted to forgive my mom. I only had one mom. Being born from an affair and not having a father, I did not want to lose my mom also. I knew she failed me and neglected me. I was angry and hurt. Maybe we would never have all that we could have had in a healthy relationship, but I wanted to forgive. As I grew older, more mature, and experienced more of life, I traveled further in the journey of forgiveness. The more I realized how truly abused, neglected, and ignored I was, the more the memories of abuse came at me like blows to my soul and slaps across my face. But every time the pain of my abuse raised its head, God's grace and mercy would meet me and surround me with peace.

There is an old expression, "How do you eat an elephant? One bite at a time." While I am not endorsing the eating of endangered species, I think this perfectly illustrates the enormity of forgiveness. Looking at the mountain of pain before you can be overwhelming. How does one forgive? Forgive what is in front of you. Small victories prepare us for larger ones. One step at a time, one victory at a time.

> *For it is precept upon precept, precept upon precept, line*
> *upon line, line upon line, here a little, there a little."*
> *- Isaiah 28:10 KJV*

I learned to trust the Lord to move the pebble and found He could also move the mountains. I wanted forgiveness in my life because I knew that was what the Lord wanted for me. He wants it for you too. I think about the story in Genesis of Jacob, whose Hebrew name means deceiver and liar. He wrestled with the angel of the Lord and did not let go until the Lord blessed him. And the Lord did bless him and gave him a new name. Jacob became Israel which means to wrestle and overcome. Just like Jacob wrestled with the angel of God, we must be willing to wrestle with our past, our pains, and our problems.

> *Then the man said, "Your name will no longer be Jacob, but Israel, because you have struggled with God and with humans and have overcome."*
>
> *- Genesis 32:28 NIV*

Often victims of abuse carry titles, names, and images that have been thrust upon them by their abuser, attacker, or even themselves. These include a hatred of oneself, insecurities, and a low self-esteem that had been instilled in them by the attacks, abuse, and shame. I know what it is like to feel like the least of these, unimportant, like dirt, a left over, a mistake, a loser. I carried those names for most of my life, but after wrestling with forgiveness and dying to self, my faith grew. I have new names. I am whole, victorious, redeemed, and set free. I am a new creation: a child of God! Today, I confess, by God's grace, I have forgiven the people who hurt and abused me.

> *For if you forgive other people when they sin against you, your heavenly Father will also forgive you.*
>
> *- Matthew 6:14 NIV*

There have been many people who didn't believe that I forgave, or who tried to minimize my testimony. One counselor even said, "I believe you believe you forgave." They were trying to qualify my testimony of forgiveness, making it an act of self will, or psychological denial of my true anger and hurt. After several months of meeting, sharing, talking, and praying, I walked into the office one afternoon and the counselor, with tears in her eyes, looked at me and said, "Mark, you truly have forgiven those who hurt you." Then she confessed, in all her years of practice, she had never met anyone who had the freedom and healing that came from complete forgiveness. That day the counselor realized forgiveness did not come by my might or power, but from the Lord.

> *Not by might nor by power, but by my Spirit,' says the Lord Almighty.*
>
> *- Zechariah 4:6 NIV*

WEIGHT LOSS

My whole life I have struggled with my weight. I have been called heavyset, husky, chunky, and big boned. I think there are a lot of reasons for that struggle. While genetics play a part, so do unhealthy habits. What was my biggest reason? I just did not care. Food was my safe place. Though my body hurt, and my health was poor, and as much as I loved my family and God, I would not let go of my unhealthy habits. I found comfort in my struggle, until the healing came.

People struggle with many different things, but for people who struggle with their weight, it is a struggle you can't hide. Culture, neighbors, sometimes even friends and family judge a person who is overweight. People assume they are lazy, unkempt, and don't care about themselves. There are reasons and excuses for their struggle, just like anyone who wrestles with other unhealthy choices.

> *For our struggle is not against flesh and blood, but against the rulers, against the authorities, against the powers of this dark world and against the spiritual forces of evil in the heavenly realms.*
>
> *- Ephesians 6:12 NIV*

For me, food always accepted me, was kind to me, and never rejected me. It was my friend. When I was hurting and my insecurities surfaced, I would punish myself with food. When I had a good day and was proud of myself, I would reward myself with food. Like any other vice, it lies to you, hurts you, and steals your hope. It promises you comfort and acceptance but can't deliver on that promise.

Ever since my early 30s, I have put myself on all kinds of diets, just like many others who wrestle with weight. Yo-yo dieting, winning some days and losing most days, was just another pain that reminded me that I was not good enough. I confessed, proclaimed, believed, and tried, but the abuse of my youth, the fears of my past, the disappointments of my life were so familiar they easily crept into my spirit and deceived me. When I did well, I was on a mountaintop, but when I did poorly, I was in a deep valley. My value was being dictated by a number on the scale. I was again in a struggle that would not only drag me back to my weakness and insecurity, but also to my old familiar friend, food. At the end of 2019 I was tired of being unhealthy, overweight, and hurting. I just wanted to get thinner. I decided to go on another weight loss program, as I had many times before. I prayed and asked the Lord to help me.

Unbeknownst to me, this time, the journey led me much deeper. It was not just about losing weight, but the reason why I was heavy and unhealthy. It helped me to understand why I found comfort in food. I had let the weight cover me, hiding the pain of what was inside. The journey would deal with the rape and molestation of my childhood. God truly opened His Word to me.

> *You, dear children, are from God and have overcome them, because the one who is in you is greater than the one who is in the world.*
>
> *- 1 John 4:4 NIV*

Again, I wish I could say the pain, hurt, and fear went away. It did not. What happened? God became bigger and stronger in my life. My confession was clearer, my faith deeper, and God's love was so much larger and greater in me than ever before. I began to love God with all that was within me. As a result, I started to love myself, because God loves me. I want to take care of myself, eat right, and exercise. I really wished a miracle had happened that night, but I did not go to bed heavy and wake up thin.

I realized the weight loss was just an expression of the deeper healing that took place in my heart, life, soul, and spirit. I have no visions of grandeur. This journey is one I need to continue every day. There will be days I do well and days I do poorly. No matter the number on the scale, no matter how I feel on a particular day or moment, I will build my life on the promise, love, and hope of God. I pray daily, asking God to remind me that my hope and peace is found in Him, my Savior. As of today, I have lost over 160 pounds, but it is only a number.

God loved me enough that He allowed me to go through the struggle, the fight, and the battle where I learned to go deeper and lean heavier on Him. He gave me the discipline and strength to lose the weight and fight the good fight. For the first time, I felt it was OK for me to be genuinely happy. I am happy getting healthier. I run and do push-ups every day. I am looking forward to running a 5k. I enjoy hiking and being outside, admiring God's amazing creation. His sanctuary is framed by pines, surrounded in granite, and refreshed with deep blue lakes and waterfalls that sing their praise to the Lord.

I am happy as I look at all the beautiful things He has created, and I am one of them. I am happy with me.

UNFORGIVENESS

In a story about forgiveness, I want to talk a little bit about what unforgiveness does. I have been around the church my whole adult life. I have met many believers who wrestled with the issue of forgiveness in their life. Forgiveness can be a challenge for a variety of reasons, as people deal with the hurt and pain of the death of a loved one, divorce, addiction, abuse, disappointments, betrayal, and regrets.

There is an earnest desire in most believers to be people who forgive those who trespass against them. The longing is real, passionate, and strong. I believe many Christians make a confession of forgiveness, stand on the scriptures, and even claim by faith their forgiveness, for Christians know what the Bible says:

> For if you forgive other people when they sin against you, your heavenly Father will also forgive you, But if you do not forgive others their sins, your Father will not forgive your sins.
>
> - *Matthew 6:14-15 NIV*

Believers so desperately want forgiveness to provide an instant release from hurt, saying, "I forgive." becomes a default response without power or promise. The desire within them to forgive is a goal that becomes louder than the reality of the process of forgiveness. God can heal in an instant, but He often walks us through the process of forgiveness. Unfortunately, if forgiveness does not fix everything quickly. Even instantly, people tend to despise the process. They have a confession of forgiveness with their lips, but still carry the pain in their spirit.

My heart breaks for the believer who confesses forgiveness, yet still holds unforgiveness within them. They are easily angered, frustrated, offended, and disappointed. This stew of unforgiveness simmers just under the surface, ready to boil over at the slightest provocation. Unforgiveness takes that stew of festering disappointment, anger, offense, fear, and frustration and then spills it out onto those we love and care for the most. This spillage takes what hurt and wounded people have in their past and projects it onto people and problems in their present. Forgiveness, on the other hand, takes those things and prevents them from being projected where they do not belong. Forgiveness helps us stand on the promises of God.

> *If we confess our sins, he is faithful and just and will forgive us our sins and purify us from all unrighteousness.*
> *- I John 1:9 NIV*

> *For if you forgive other people when they sin against you, your heavenly Father will also forgive you.*
> *- Matthew 6:14 NIV*

The process of forgiveness can be ugly, difficult, and honest at the same time. We must often inspect our heart and deal with the unforgiveness found within. It's not about those who offended, hurt, or broke us. It is about us and God. Admitting the anger, hurt, and hate we carry is difficult. How can I feel anger, hatred, pain, disappointment, fear, and frustration and still praise God? God loves you. His word is true, His altar is available, and He tells us:

> *"Come to me, all you who are weary and burdened, and I will give you rest. Take my yoke upon you and learn from me, for I am gentle and humble in heart, and you will find rest for your souls. For my yoke is easy and my burden is light."*
>
> *- Matthew 11:28-30 NIV*

God does not reject those dealing with unforgiveness. Your heavenly father knows you, and He wants you to come.

> *Cast all your anxiety on Him because He cares for you.*
> *- 1 Peter 5:7 NIV*

He wants to walk with you and accompany you on the journey of forgiveness. Are you sad? He will weep with you.

> *Jesus wept.*
> *- John 11:35 NIV*

Are you weak? He will make you strong.

> *But He said to me, "My grace is sufficient for you, for my power is made perfect in weakness." Therefore I will boast all the more gladly about my weaknesses, so that Christ's power may rest on me. That is why, for Christ's sake, I delight in weaknesses, in insults, in hardships, in persecutions, in difficulties. For when I am weak, then I am strong.*
>
> *- 2 Corinthians 12:9-10 NIV*

The process is necessary. Go through the process. Be real with God. Pray, cry, worship, sing, or write. Never forget that the Lord will never leave you nor forsake you. Your forgiveness is a journey, and the Lord will be with you always.

"Never will I leave you; never will I forsake you."
- Hebrews 13:5b NIV

The following are some insightful truths Dr. Sam Storm has given to the church about the reality of forgiveness. They were impactful to me, and I trust they will guide you as well.

Five Myths about Forgiveness
1. Contrary to what many have been led to believe, forgiveness is not forgetting.
2. Forgiving someone does not mean you no longer feel the pain of their offense.
3. Forgiving someone who has sinned against you doesn't mean you cease longing for justice.
4. Forgiveness does not mean you are to make it easy for the offender to hurt you again.
5. Forgiveness is rarely a one-time, climactic event.

Five Truths About Forgiveness
1. God in Christ forgave us by absorbing in Himself the destructive and painful consequences of our sin against Him.
2. God forgave us in Christ by canceling the debt we owed Him. That is to say, we are no longer held liable for our sins or in any way made to pay for them.
3. Forgiving others as God has forgiven us means we resolve to revoke revenge.

4. Forgiving others as God has forgiven us means that we determine to do good to them rather than evil.

5. God forgave us in Christ by reconciling us to Himself, by restoring the relationship that our sin had shattered.

Often on our journey to forgiveness we are faced with questions, emotions, perspectives, and philosophies. As we think on such thoughts and try to articulate them, while also trying to navigate and comprehend the injustice that was done to us, we study and pray trying to find help through it all. We look for others that have walked the same road. We surround ourselves with wise teachers and learn from insightful writers. All of Dr Sam Storm's words ring true to me. They echo and capture the expression of my own understanding. He truly articulated the nuances of forgiveness in a most complete and concise way.

GOD IS BIGGER

Insecurity and fear lie to the broken and can affect people in two different ways. Some retreat within themselves, afraid to share their opinions frightened to stand up, or take control. They are comfortable in the shadows, allowing others to lead even when they know they're wrong. Fear, doubt, and shame remind them, "You can't. You are never right." Others promote themselves. They are the kind of people who know everybody and have done everything. Their insecurities cry out see, respect what I have, who I know and what I have done. Yet that same person hopes no one sees who they really are or notices the depths of their doubt.

People who walk through hurts often long for the moment the pain, regret, and fear will be vanquished. They wait for the day they're not haunted by their past. They find themselves negotiating with God, "I will go where you tell me. I will do what you call me to do, but first take this issue in my life away." The past raises its head and tries to limit our future, our potential, and our hope.

In my life, I have met very few people for whom God has instantly removed their hurts and pains, healing them in a moment. God does not remove the past. He makes a way through the problems and fears to bring forgiveness. In the book of Genesis, Moses was standing on the edge of the Red Sea, surrounded by trouble. His enemies were behind him, and a major obstacle was in front of him. God didn't remove the enemies; He didn't remove the obstacle. He made a way through them.

> *Then Moses stretched out his hand over the sea, and all*
> *that night the Lord drove the sea back with a strong east*
> *wind and turned it into dry land. The waters were divided,*
> *and the Israelites went through the sea on dry ground, with*
> *a wall of water on their right and on their left.*
> *- Exodus 14:21-22 NIV*

I wish I could write to you today and tell you that my past hurts are gone. That the familiar insecurities, fears, and troubles never try to drag me down or control me, but they do. The past never stops whispering in my ear, but I have learned that God is always bigger. Bigger than the mountain of hurts.

As I started to get healthy and began losing weight, I challenged myself to do something that I had not done in a long time. I went for a hike, just to be outside and enjoy nature. There is a small mountain not too far from our house. It was just a moderate half-mile hike, but at that time, that mountain seemed like Everest to me. I gathered my family and some friends and off we went. It was a great challenge . It took me over two hours to climb to the top and back. I was proud to complete that hike and grateful to my friends and family who walked with me. I had blisters on my feet and bruises on my toes, but I did it!

A few months later, as my health journey continued, I had lost a significant amount of weight. I was challenged and guided by a friend, who is an avid climber. Together we climbed the highest peak in the state of New York – Mt. Marcy. The climb took two days, and it was fourteen miles round-trip. I was enormously proud to successfully tackle that mountain.

The first mountain, as big as it was to me at the time, was small in comparison to the second mountain. I know your current mountain may seem insurmountable, but God will get you through and you will look back, thankful to see how far God has brought you. God became bigger in my life, and He will become bigger in yours, too.

> *I lift up my eyes to the mountains—where does my help come from? My help comes from the Lord, the Maker of heaven and earth.*
>
> *- Psalm 121:1-2 NIV*

In the shadow of the Lord, I have grown in confidence, faith, and trust before God and man. Confidence was the greatest thing the abuse had stolen from me. Learning to live in confidence, I feel like the student that has learned a new skill. I feel like a builder with a new tool. I know this confidence comes from the Lord. It did not originate within me, but through the power of the Holy Spirit.

> *For the Lord will be your confidence,*
> *And will keep your foot from being caught.*
> *- Proverbs 3:26 NKJV*

I feel like I have come out of the shadow and into the light. Before, I felt invisible — but now I feel like I can be seen and let my light shine. My voice was silent, my opinion did not matter, but now I am more aware of my reason and purpose to be a witness, share my testimony and praise the Lord.

> *So do not fear, for I am with you; do not be dismayed, for I am your God. I will strengthen you and help you; I will uphold you with my righteous right hand.*
> *- Isaiah 41:10 NIV*

God is bigger than the past. God is bigger than your past.

PART II
| TRAIL MARKERS |

ABOUT TRAIL MARKERS

"What are your action steps?" is a popular question asked by many life coaches and counselors. This question encourages people toward introspection, helping them evaluate their motives and desires, to formulate goals and changes needed to navigate their life and choices. On my journey of forgiving the nightmare, I saw my steps, goals, and reflections wrapped up in the image of trail markers.

> *Show me your ways, Lord, teach me your paths. Guide me in your truth and teach me, for you are God my Savior, and my hope is in you all day long.*
>
> *- Psalm 25:4-5 NIV*

Every hiker knows that sometimes everything starts to look the same and you ask yourself "Have I been here before? Gone past that tree? Climbed that rock? Crossed this valley?" There is often a moment of panic or anxiety when you believe you have strayed from the trail and are lost. This is when you look for the trail markers to help you find your way. Every state and trail system has its own kind of trail markers that vary in size color and shape. It is important to be able to identify the correct marker that will lead you to your destination.

There are often places where paths will cross, or places where paths intertwine, sometimes sharing the same trail for short distances or many miles. You must be careful here as you identify your trail markers, or you could end up following the wrong path. It is easy to get distracted by many things at this point. Whether it is the ease or difficulty of the path, or the enjoyment of company you are with. When many people are sharing the same path, it is easy to connect, get talking, become distracted, and lose your way.

Whoever walks with the wise becomes wise,
but the companion of fools will suffer harm.
- Proverbs 13:20 ESV

Sometimes the path is noticeably clear and well-traveled, and the need to pay attention to the trail markers may seem to be less important. It is easier to walk this path because you are following in the footsteps of those who have gone before you. Other times the path is not so clear, maybe because you are tired, or it could be covered with leaves or snow. Finding the correct trail marker reassures you and restores your confidence that you are on the right path.

God gives us trail markers that identify the paths He has marked out for us. They evoke the same security and confidence of knowing you are on the right path. On my journey from hurting and broken to hope and freedom, there were also trail markers. There were people and Scriptures that helped me evaluate where I was along the way. The trail markers that God gave me were spiritual. The Lord placed His word, faith, and individuals in my life to challenge and guide me along the way.

The following are my trail markers. They are the challenging questions I ask myself, and God, to stay focused on what is ahead. Some days I struggle to find the trail markers and get lost, confused, or turned around. Other days they are much clearer, marking the way. There are times on the journey when you feel like you are traveling from marker to marker and not making any real progress. Stay on track. Don't give up. Follow the trail markers, and with every step you take you will get closer to reaching the summit, attaining your goal, and arriving at your destination. When you are tired, in doubt, or feel you have lost your way, may you hear God's Word saying:

Whether you turn to the right or to the left, your ears will hear a voice behind you, saying, "This is the way; walk in it."

- Isaiah 30:21 NIV

TRAIL MARKER 1: PRAYER

I've heard prayer defined many ways. Some were scholarly and others were simple. The definition I like best is that prayer is simply talking to God. There are lofty prayers with deep theological terms and simple prayers, some just a guttural cry of help. Prayers can be long, or short, passionate or rehearsed. No matter the form, length, or intensity, prayer in its purest form is when we just talk to God.

We pour ourselves out to God rehearsing countless topics through prayer. We deeply inspect ourselves before God, crying out for Him to meet our needs, wants, and desires. We ask, "Why?" as we search our past and look with hope to our future. We submit. We surrender. We pick up. We run. We let go. We say yes. We say no. We cry. We laugh. We are silent. We seek and we find. We pray.

> *Hear my prayer, O God; listen to the words of my mouth.*
> *- Psalm 54:2 NIV*

Talking to God always felt natural to me. My prayer life has never been super formal. It has always been raw, honest, and genuine. Smith Wigglesworth is quoted as saying, "I don't often spend more than half an hour in prayer at one time, but I never go more than half an hour without praying. That statement sums up my prayer life. I've prayed out of desperation, excitement, joy, and fear. I've prayed for my needs, my loved ones, my family, and my enemies. I have often examined my prayer life. Was I praying for my own gain or God's glory? Was I asking God to change others or change me? Was I going to God as a cosmic Santa Claus, or as my heavenly father?

All my life I've been told I talk too much. I have had nicknames like motormouth and foghorn. Those names have followed me around my whole life. My mom used to say to me, "Markie, you will either grow up to be a filibuster or a preacher." My family says that I talk to anyone. Some people say I even talk to the walls. For me it was never a question about talking to God. The question for me has always been, "Is God really listening?"

As I grew in my relationship with the Lord, when I was in a place of prayer, vulnerable and genuine, I would wonder, "Does God, Creator of all, King of kings and Lord of lords hear me? Does God really hear and care about me? Will He really guide and direct me? Or am I just talking to myself about my fears, wants, and dreams? Am I praying to a God who hears me, loves me, and cares about me? Can I trust the Lord?" One of the hardest things for me to deal with as a result of the abuse, and one of the last things that was restored to me, was trust. Trust in myself, trust in others, and most of all trust in God.

> *I will say of the Lord, "He is my refuge and my fortress,*
> *my God, in whom I trust."*
> *- Psalm 91:2 NIV*

Trust means letting others into your life, Trust is allowing others to see your secrets, your mistakes, your fears. Before I could tell my wife I loved her, before I asked for her hand in marriage, I said, "I trust you." Prayer is where you learn to trust God. Trusting God is where you learn to pray. Prayer is where are you learn to listen to God and sometimes it is really hard to be quiet and still and just listen. Learning to hear the voice of the Lord from all the other thoughts, distractions, and noises clamoring for attention. Learning to trust His voice, being quiet and still long enough to hear it.

> *My sheep listen to my voice; I know them, and they follow me.*
>
> *- John 10:27 NIV*

> *In the past God spoke to our ancestors through the prophets at many times and in various ways, but in these last days he has spoken to us by his Son, whom he appointed heir of all things, and through whom also he made the universe.*
>
> *- Hebrews1:1-2 NIV*

Prayer is real! God still speaks to us today. We can learn to recognize His voice as we read His Word, the Bible. God is real and He wants to talk with you!

> *You have searched me, Lord, and you know me. You know when I sit and when I rise; you perceive my thoughts from afar. You discern my going out and my lying down; you are familiar with all my ways. Before a word is on my tongue you, Lord, know it completely. You hem me in behind and before, and you lay your hand upon me. Such knowledge is too wonderful for me too lofty for me to attain.*
>
> *- Psalm 139:1-6 NIV*

During prayer God will speak to you, encourage you, rebuke you, and challenge you. God's voice will become so clear to you it will ring in your heart and mind. You will learn to know the Word of the Lord because it will line up with the Bible. At times it will be a comfort, other times it will challenge you. As you pray and get to know God more, you can walk humbly but with confidence. Realize how weak you are, yet how strong God is. God will move in ways you can only imagine. When storms come, doubt creeps in, and your body is weak that still small voice of the Lord calls and beckons you to draw closer to the Lord.

> Let us then approach God's throne of grace with confidence, so that we may receive mercy and find grace to help us in our time of need.
>
> *- Hebrews 4:16 NIV*

This is when trust brings you back to prayer and prayer bring you back to trust in the Lord.

At times on your journey, during the intimacy of prayer, the Lord will call, ask, and inspire you out of love for God to forgive others from your past, even your nightmare. The Lord will say, "You are ready, you can do it, you can forgive." You may get angry, scared, and fight against it, but through prayer you can find the strength to take that first step toward forgiveness. Through prayer God can change you and heal you from the inside out. Prayer can change your perspective and countenance.

> And when you stand praying, if you hold anything against anyone, forgive them, so that your Father in heaven may forgive you your sins."
>
> *- Mark 11:25 NIV*

For I know the plans I have for you," declares the Lord, "plans to prosper you and not to harm you, plans to give you hope and a future. Then you will call on me and come and pray to me, and I will listen to you. You will seek me and find me when you seek me with all your heart.
- Jeremiah 29:11-13

Take time daily to pray and seek the Lord for His strength, and grace to forgive. Hold tight to the Lord as He takes you by the hand and helps you to forgive, let go, and surrender.

Let the first trail marker of prayer to the Lord guide you as He gives you strength, hope, and peace for your journey.

TRAIL MARKER 2: BIBLE

The Bible is the written Word of God. I have quite a unique relationship when it comes to reading. Reading for me has never been enjoyable. It has always been a discipline. When it comes to reading, I choose to make the effort to read although it is not something I find pleasure in, nor do I find it relaxing.

Growing up in abuse there were many casualties and one of the casualties was my education. I've struggled with dyslexia all my life. In that struggle, at times I've been embarrassed, frustrated, and ashamed. There were days when I tried to read but the insecurities were so loud, and inabilities so evident, the last thing I wanted to do was read. Attempts at reading reinforced my feelings of inadequacy, as I battled the fears of feeling like a failure. Reading the Bible felt like an unclimbable mountain, the summit too high and the path too rough to even attempt.

> *Let me understand the teaching of your precepts; then I will meditate on your wonders. My soul is weary with sorrow; strengthen me according to your word.*
> *- Psalm 119:27-28*

I would remind myself, "This is God's Holy Word, all I need to do is read it, understand it, and apply it." I would find a safe place where I could open the Bible and find a Scripture. I would start trying to read, but my poor reading skills consistently derailed my efforts. I would shut the book and walk away defeated. I had a desire in my heart to read but I did not have the ability, patience, or fortitude to persevere. Feeling more broken than when I started, I would walk away. Yet, I knew that God had given us His Word in written form. God tells us the Word became flesh and it also tells us that the Word of the Lord will not perish.

> *In the beginning was the Word, and the Word was with God, and the Word was God.*
> *- John 1:1 NIV*

> *As the rain and the snow come down from heaven, and do not return to it without watering the earth and making it bud and flourish, so that it yields seed for the sower and bread for the eater, so is my word that goes out from my mouth: It will not return to me empty, but will accomplish what I desire and achieve the purpose for which I sent it.*
> *- Isaiah 55:10-11 NIV*

How I longed to get to know God through His Word not just what people told me about God. I wanted to read it for myself. I wanted to understand. I genuinely wanted to know the Bible, to discover, study, and stand on its truth. God had chosen to speak to His people through His written Word, yet I felt empty because I did not have the ability to read or understand it. While I knew the Lord would enlighten me and convict me, I felt for the longest time that maybe the Bible wasn't for me. I was stuck, caught up in this vortex of broken understanding.

*For the word of God is alive and active... it judges the
thoughts and attitudes of the heart.*
- Hebrews 4:12 NIV

Then I felt God convicting me as He challenged my motives. Did I
want to use the Bible as a hammer to get my point across, to be
right, and feel superior, while not allowing the Bible to pierce my
heart and bring me closer to God? Was I studying the Bible daily,
applying it to my life to become stronger and gain the knowledge
and the wisdom of God? Now, as I read His Word I am filled with
a desire to be more like Christ, to learn, understand, and hear His
voice calling me. As I have studied the Bible and allowed His Word
to pierce through my defenses, insecurities, and pain to soften my
heart, His Word changed me.

*I will give you a new heart and put a new spirit in you; I
will remove from you your heart of stone and give you a
heart of flesh. And I will put my Spirit in you and move
you to follow my decrees and be careful to keep my laws.*
- Ezekiel 36:26-27 NIV

God's Word, directs us, convicts us, and strengthens us. God uses
His Word to speak to our hearts, fill our mind with understanding
and our mouth with wisdom. Some days I am able to read more
easily than others, but I try to read a little every day. Some days I
feel like I could conquer many chapters and other days I can only
manage a few words. I believe God has increased my understanding of His Word more and more. As God teaches me through His
Word I understand more of His love, mercy, and grace.

Your word is a lamp for my feet, a light on my path.
- Psalm 119:105 NIV

He has filled me with a passion to preach His Word. The Word of God is full of truth, direction, understanding, and wisdom. The Word promises hope, love, grace, and mercy. Reading is still a chore for me to this day. I have let go of the insecurities of my youth and accepted my inabilities knowing I may never be the strong reader I want to be. By God's grace, I refuse to allow my poor reading to steal the gift of God's Word. When I read, I feel like a thirsty man longing for something to drink, longing for my thirst to be satisfied. God's Word is more satisfying than silver or gold it satisfies all that is within me.

> *As the deer pants for streams of water, so my soul pants for you, my God.*
>
> *- Psalm 42:1*

Sometimes I feel like I am reading on a timer just waiting for the dyslexia to catch up and break the momentum of what I am reading. This makes me read intentionally with passion and intensity as I try to absorb and understand everything I have just read. It is in these moments when I can read clearly that I have gotten some of my strongest rebukes and biggest blessings.

As a trail marker God's Word helps me stay on the path God has called me to walk. It reminds me of what God can do and gives me confidence. It keeps me sober minded and reminds me that I am loved and accepted. It humbles me and reminds me that I am still working out my salvation with fear and trembling. God's Word is beautiful, difficult, challenging, and a blessing. God still uses His Words to speak to His people. God is still using His Word to speak to you and me.

Let the Word of God guide you and keep you on your journey.

TRAIL MARKER 3: FAITH

Now faith is confidence in what we hope for and assurance about what we do not see.

- Hebrews 11:1 NIV

The early years of my life were challenging. I lived in brokenness and knew nothing but dysfunction. I was a walking example of regret, shame, pain, sorrow, and hurt. Faith was a distant concept. The people I grew up with had more faith that a dog would treat them right than they did in any person, church, or even God.

Faith was hard concept to grasp. I did not hope, I wished. I wished certain things would happen. I wished I could have what I lacked, I wished certain feelings would go away. Looking back, I now know that faith is so much more than a wish. It is hope. Hope that is not built on my abilities or my desires. It is a hope that is found in a relationship with God. Faith is not just desiring an attribute, position, or possession. Faith is turning your eyes, heart and will to the Lord, trusting and believing that the Lord your God will make a way or open a door, not always of your choosing, but the one that will be the right one for you to go through.

We wait in hope for the Lord; he is our help and our shield. In him our hearts rejoice, for we trust in his holy name. May your unfailing love be with us, Lord, even as we put our hope in you.

- Psalm 33:20-22 NIV

On the journey of forgiveness, there are attacks from the enemy. The arrows can cut deep and ring true. It is so easy to bend and succumb to the attacks when we focus on them. Even though the enemy has lost the war he tries to win as many skirmishes as he can. His goal is to inflict as much pain as possible. The enemy wants to steal, kill, and destroy. The enemy lies as he tries to pull us down and hold us back from the hope we have in Christ. Just as a soldier has armor to protect himself during a battle, God has given us what we need to protect us from the enemy.

Therefore put on the full armor of God, so that when the day of evil comes, you may be able to stand your ground, and after you have done everything, to stand. Stand firm then, with the belt of truth buckled around your waist, with the breastplate of righteousness in place, and with your feet fitted with the readiness that comes from the gospel of peace. In addition to all this, take up the shield of faith, with which you can extinguish all the flaming arrows of the evil one. Take the helmet of salvation and the sword of the Spirit, which is the word of God. And pray in the Spirit on all occasions with all kinds of prayers and requests. With this in mind, be alert and always keep on praying for all the Lord's people.

- Ephesians 6:13-18 NIV

God gives us faith as a tool to be a shield about us to quench the fiery arrows of the enemy. Faith in God gives me the hope, strength, and belief that God is with me through every attack. Faith in God teaches me that I will not always get my way, but God will always make a way to glorify Himself through me. When we doubt we must call out to God and remember the things He has done, thanking Him for all His blessings. In that moment, faith rises like an early morning sunrise when the sun first crests over the horizon. Through the first rays of light the brightness of the sun pushes out all the darkness, surrounding you with the warmth and the promise of a new day.

> *Give praise to the Lord, proclaim his name; make known among the nations what he has done. Sing to him, sing praise to him; tell of all his wonderful acts. Glory in his holy name; let the hearts of those who seek the Lord rejoice. Look to the Lord and his strength; seek his face always.*
>
> *- Psalm 105:1-4 NIV*

Faith rises in me in the face of my insecurities, fears, inabilities, and the lies of the enemy. I walk by faith and not by sight. Faith tells me my God is with me. I am forgiven and I can forgive. Through faith I can overcome, climb the next mountain, walk through the next valley. In those moments when the enemy tries to come in to steal, kill, and destroy, I know my God is with me.

> *Be strong and courageous. Do not be afraid or terrified because of them, for the Lord your God goes with you; he will never leave you nor forsake you."*
>
> *- Deuteronomy 31:6 NIV*

I am saved by grace, but I walk by faith. When doubt creeps in, my hope in God causes my faith to rise. When fear surrounds me, threatening to choke out my purpose and promise, faith pushes the fear away. Faith starts small, like a mustard seed. The mustard seed is tiny, yet it grows to be such a large plant that birds build nests in its shade. As we put our hope in God and lift our eyes to Him, our faith in God grows.

> *"Lord, if it's you," Peter replied, "tell me to come to you on the water."*
> *"Come," he said. Then Peter got down out of the boat, walked on the water and came toward Jesus. But when he saw the wind, he was afraid and, beginning to sink, cried out, "Lord, save me!" Immediately Jesus reached out his hand and caught him. "You of little faith," he said, "why did you doubt?" And when they climbed into the boat, the wind died down.*
>
> *- Matthew 14:28-32 NIV*

As we allow faith in God to fill our heart and our mind, our faith grows and doubts become quieter as we walk in the confidence that only faith in God can give us. This faith reminds us God will make a way and helps us stand on the belief that the Lord will do what is right. He will give us what we need and will be glorified through the storm, tragedy, or pain. God is the same God on the mountaintop as He is in the valley. God is the same whether we have plenty or nothing at all.

> *Even though I walk through the valley of the shadow of death, I will fear no evil, for you are with me; your rod and your staff, they comfort me.*
>
> *- Psalm 23:4 NIV*

When Jesus talks about faith He encourages us to believe. Belief and faith grow stronger the more they are exercised, the same way that our muscles get stronger the more we use them. However, we must be careful where we put our faith. Sometimes the zeal to move, experience, and express our life-changing faith can take us to places which may be difficult to navigate. We desire to have a passionate, world changing faith, and as believers we can have that kind of faith. Yet, our faith must not be directed toward the outcome of our desire. Our faith must trust God's will in every circumstance. It is not about receiving; it is about becoming. It is about yielding our desires to God's will. Faith in ourselves, or in other people, will eventually fail. God will not.

> *"Father, if you are willing, take this cup from me; yet not my will, but yours be done."*
>
> *- Luke 22:42 NIV*

Faith tells us we can trust in the Word of God. The Word tells us that God has a plan. He is working all things for our good and His glory and honor. Our faith in God beckons us to draw closer to God, giving us the strength to trust Him as He leads us to see things through His perspective. As we reach out to God and study His Word, He reminds us of His faithfulness, it rings in our ears as faith erupts in our soul. Trust in the Lord, see the goodness and the sweetness of His grace. Know when we stumble, God picks us up, strengthens our faith, and points us in the right direction on our journey. Faith in God is never misplaced, even when we do not receive what we think we should. God's plans are more far reaching than we can imagine. It may not be until we see Him in heaven that we understand what His plans were. Let us walk by faith and let faith in God be a significant Trail Marker on our path.

> *For the word of the Lord is right and true; he is faithful in all he does.*
>
> *- Psalm 33:4 NIV*

TRAIL MARKER 4: LOVE

"A new command I give you: Love one another. As I have loved you, so you must love one another."

- John 13:34 NIV

God is love. What a beautiful expression that captures hope, passion, and acceptance. On my path to forgiveness, I had to discover what real love was. I had to determine if my love for God and others was conditional. Did I love only because I received something in return? Or had I learned to love unselfishly, sacrificially, and truly?

For someone who grew up in a home full of brokenness, dysfunction, and pain, love often meant self-preservation. It meant placing my needs over the needs of anyone else. My understanding about love was dependent upon whether I got what I wanted or how I felt about a situation or person. People can misuse love, twisting it into something unhealthy, abusive, selfish, demanding, and controlling. For many of us who grew up with abuse, this twisted version of love was not only demonstrated to us, it was considered normal. This broken version of what I interpreted to be love was demanding, compelling me to perform, or hold back. As a child it was the only love I knew, but it was not real love. Real love is a gift that respects, cares, and protects unselfishly.

> *Love is patient, love is kind. It does not envy, it does not boast, it is not proud. It does not dishonor others, it is not self-seeking, it is not easily angered, it keeps no record of wrongs. Love does not delight in evil but rejoices with the truth. It always protects, always trusts, always hopes, always perseveres.*
>
> *- 1 Corinthians 13:4-7 NIV*

There were times in my life when I behaved foolishly, or acted a part to find acceptance and love, only to walk away feeling more rejected and unloved than when I started. I was angry at myself for how I acted, becoming a caricature of who I truly was. I believed for many years that if I was good enough, if I did what people said, then maybe they would love me. Not only was it exhausting, it lead to anger, frustration, and self-loathing.

Jesus taught us to love our neighbors like we love ourselves. This is what I did. I loved my neighbors like I loved myself, with high demands, selfish expectations, and unrealistic standards. Because it was the kind of love I knew, it was the kind of love I gave.

> *The Lord appeared to us in the past, saying: "I have loved you with an everlasting love; I have drawn you with unfailing kindness.*
>
> *- Jeremiah 31:3 NIV*

> *This is how God showed his love among us: He sent his one and only Son into the world that we might live through him. This is love: not that we loved God, but that he loved us and sent his Son as an atoning sacrifice for our sins.*
>
> *- 1 John 4:9-10 NIV*

When Christ became my Savior, I was told that He loved me and because He loved me, He died for me. That kind of love was strange and foreign to me. I was convinced that love always came with conditions. As a young, broken kid, I could not comprehend unconditional love. While I did not understand it, I sure did want it. The love of God melted away my misunderstandings, poor examples, and the lies about love that were demonstrated to me. God was taking my heart of stone and making it a heart of flesh. The magnitude of the love of God overwhelmed me. I would weep at the altar in the middle of worship, not knowing where the tears and emotions were coming from. It was one of the first times I felt accepted. God's love is true.

> *And I am convinced that nothing can ever separate us from God's love. Neither death nor life, neither angels nor demons, neither our fears for today nor our worries about tomorrow—not even the powers of hell can separate us from God's love.*
>
> *- Romans 8:38 NLT*

Before I could love and forgive others, I had to love God. In loving God, I learned to love my neighbor, my brother, and myself. I learned that God's love is unchanging and does not depend on what He gets from us, and neither should our love for others depend on what we get from them. God loved us before we knew Him. Nothing we do affects His love for us. That knowledge overwhelmed me, amazed me, built me up, made me new, and supported me.

> *The LORD your God is with you, he is mighty to save. He will take great delight in you, he will quiet you with his love, he will rejoice over you with singing.*
>
> *- Zephaniah 3:17 NIV, 1984*

When Jesus called Peter to step out of the boat and walk on water, as long as Peter was focused on Jesus, he could do the impossible. As soon as he took his eyes off the Lord and focused on the circumstances around him, he started to sink into the waves. How do you love? How do you forgive? By keeping your eyes, your gaze, your faith, focused on Jesus Christ.

> *Be kind and compassionate to one another, forgiving each other, just as in Christ God forgave you.*
> *- Ephesians 4:32 NIV*

God is love. May the trail marker of God's love fill you and wash over you as you continue on your journey.

TRAIL MARKER 5: TRUST

"But blessed is the one who trusts in the Lord, whose confidence is in him.

- Jeremiah 17:7 NIV

Was I truly trusting God, or myself, my emotions, and my feelings? Was I vulnerable, allowing myself to believe and trust God and others? Were my decisions based on my best, or God's best for my life?

For those of us who have been through trauma trust is one of those areas that is a constant challenge. When you have been broken, lied to, hurt, and manipulated, it becomes difficult to trust God and others. You become skeptical of others waiting for them to let you down, or for yet another traumatic experience to knock you down. Why? Because abandonment, the lack of commitment, support, and protection, weakens the trust we have for others. It also weakens the trust we have in our self. Trusting others fully became one of the biggest mountains I had to climb. I was betrayed so many times by people who said they loved me. I adopted that old saying as my life's mantra, "Fool me once shame on you. Fool me twice shame on me." I was not mean or cruel, I just did not trust.

What they trust in is fragile; what they rely on is a spider's web. They lean on the web, but it gives way; they cling to it, but it does not hold.

- Job 8:14-15 NIV

I remember moments when I genuinely wanted to trust someone, but I would talk myself out of it because I was afraid of getting hurt again. It was lonely behind the emotional walls I had built, but it also felt safe. I allowed some in, but I stayed relationally distant. I am a social person and enjoy hearing people's stories, but something always held me back from getting too connected. I would consciously or subconsciously sabotage the friendship, or fracture the relationship, just because I was afraid of trusting them.

My wall was tall and impenetrable, and my justifications for why it was right not to trust were even bigger. I felt safe but alone in my fortress of doubt and fear. I felt like I needed the wall to keep me safe and protected. It was my constant reminder to never let anyone get so close they could hurt me. I held onto this belief with religious fervor.

When I am afraid, I put my trust in you.
- Psalm 56:3 NIV

During that time, I would describe my friendships as novelty items. A novelty is something that is initially fun, like a new toy. You play with it, you show it off, and you tell others about it. The appeal of the novelty quickly subsides, and the cycle starts again. You stop talking about it and it sits on a shelf and collects dust. What I didn't see is that I also became the novelty. People didn't abandon our friendship because they were mean. I pushed them away and retreated to my fortress of solitude. I was alone, once again, but felt safe.

> *Those who trust in themselves are fools, but those who walk*
> *in wisdom are kept safe.*
>
> *- Proverbs 28:26 NIV*

The Bible tells us to test all things and hold fast to what is good. I was testing, but not holding on to the good. When following a trail marker, GPS, or map, you are trusting the one who went before you; the one who made the path and planned the way. They marked the dangerous terrain and risked their lives to protect those who would follow, so you trust them with your life. Following a trail marker, GPS, or map leaves you vulnerable, open, and susceptible as you trust those who went before you. Every map is only as good as the person who created it. In our journey to forgiveness Jesus has blazed the trail, and He has left us a reliable guide and a map – the Holy Spirit and the Bible.

> *May the God of hope fill you with all joy and peace as you*
> *trust in him, so that you may overflow with hope by the*
> *power of the Holy Spirit.*
>
> *- Romans 15:13*

God also provides people to encourage us on our journey. People are not perfect. We all know that, but what I expected from others was birthed from fear not from friendship. Learning to trust was a slow, arduous process that took patience, both in God and in myself. I'm still learning to trust in God's love, mercy, and His Word. I was still vulnerable, but this time I chose to be vulnerable before the Lord. It was in that place of vulnerability where the Holy Spirit taught me to trust others. Only by keeping the Lord first can I find the hope to overcome the great fear of trusting others.

He put a new song in my mouth, a hymn of praise to our God. Many will see and fear the Lord and put their trust in him.

- Psalm 40:3

It is beautiful when someone who only knew mistrust and betrayal begins to trust. This did not take place over night. It took years. This newfound trust can be fragile and easily spooked. It can be forgotten and pushed away. Like most things we learn, it started small and slowly grew. There is not a moment where you say, "I got it." or "I have arrived." One day you will notice that trusting God has become a natural part of you in your words, actions, and deeds.

May trust be another trail marker on your journey. Stand firm and walk strong as you trust in God!

TRAIL MARKER 6: FRIENDS

> *I no longer call you servants, because a servant does not know his master's business. Instead, I have called you friends, for everything that I learned from my Father I have made known to you.*
>
> *- John 15:15 NIV*

Were friends just a means to an end to get what I want? Was I truly aware of what it meant to be a friend? Was I the kind of friend I hoped to be? Was I allowing Christ to call me friend?

> *One who has unreliable friends soon comes to ruin, but there is a friend who sticks closer than a brother.*
>
> *- Proverbs 18:24 NIV*

Friends can be both a great blessing and a great source of struggle. God used many of my friends to be trail markers, helping me along my journey. It is not always easy being a friend with someone who has been abused. I wanted friends, but first I needed to learn how to *be* a friend. My experiences taught me how to survive and protect myself from feelings of abandonment and rejection. It took me a while to figure out that being a friend has nothing to do with manipulation.

I had been a chameleon, blending in and moving on from one friend to another. I always needed people in my life to keep from feeling alone, yet it wouldn't be long before I pushed them away. I morphed into the person I thought the people around me needed, betraying myself in the process.

What a facade. What a sham. I was still alone. I was a collection of fractured identities and unhealthy perspectives. I was a dysfunctional blend of the expectations of the people around me. I thought if I could be what people wanted me to be, if I could say what people wanted me to say, that I would be accepted and liked.

Unfortunately, I was not as good a friend to those who were trying to befriend me, simply because I did not know how to be a friend. At least, not the kind of friend that loves at all times. I thank the Lord for the people who were really friends to me despite my failures. As I sit here, I think of those real friends in my life. We were all kids, trying to figure out life and our walk with the Lord. Those friends surrounded me and taught me what real friendship was through their love, actions, and example.

> *Perfume and incense bring joy to the heart, and the pleasantness of a friend springs from their heartfelt advice.*
> *- Proverbs 27:9*

I thank God for my friends who called me out and held me to a higher standard. Friends who were patient and demanded that I show the real me. Those moments where I was challenged to grow were not always easy, but they were needed. They were filled with passion, expectations, and honesty. There were fiery words, but their goals were clear. Knock "it" off. Give "it" up. Their commitment was just as deep. They were on my side and had my back.

As iron sharpens iron, so one person sharpens another.
- Proverbs 27:17

I did not realize it at the time, but a bunch of young people taught me how to be an adult. I was taught the value and commitment of true friendship and I am thankful. Those friends today have lives, careers, and families. While we often don't see each other for months, or maybe years at a time, when we get together it is like the months and years are only moments. Those friends invested in me and sowed into me because of our friendship. God has used friendships to speak to me, call me out, and confirm God's Word in my life. An isolated man can convince himself of almost anything, that his actions are pure, and his motives are always right. But a man with friends has a sounding board and a council for wisdom. A true friend can talk to you like no one else can. They tell you when you are being unkind, dishonest, unreasonable, or falling short, and say it in a way that declares, "I love you."

I needed friends and most of all I longed to *be* a friend. There are people who come and go. Then there are people who you share life with and are a part of your community. They get you, even when you are being foolish, and forgive you when you make mistakes. They are friends who will be with you through sorrow and rejoice with you in seasons of celebration. Friends who will encourage you and tell you the truth even when you do not want to hear it.

> *I thank my God every time I remember you. In all my prayers for all of you, I always pray with joy because of your partnership in the gospel from the first day until now, being confident of this, that he who began a good work in you will carry it on to completion until the day of Christ Jesus.*
>
> *- Philippians 1:3-6*

Lord, thank you for being a friend that sticks closer than a brother. Thank you for showing me how to be a friend. Thank you for giving me friends. Lord, I pray and ask that you will bless my friends with your love and mercy. I pray they all grow closer to you. I pray that you help me be a friend. The kind of friend that will support, love, and speak truth and hope. Amen.

Friendship is a trail marker that God has given us. He has given us the gift of people, placing them in our lives to help us on our journey.

TRAIL MARKER 7: FREEDOM

Do I keep my voice quiet enough, my emotions small enough, and my reactions low enough to break free from my excuses? Do I make myself decrease and let others increase by not being the center of attention, the one that needs to speak every time? Do I let God's grace lead me and not let my insecurities drive me?

> Be *completely humble and gentle; be patient, bearing with one another in love.*
>
> *- Ephesians 4:2 NIV*

The trail marker of freedom starts with honesty. My daughters often sing a song around the house. In that song is a line that says, "being honest is the only way to fix it". How true. I had a lot of pain, anger, and frustration. For many years, I was a victim to my abuser, to my circumstances, to the broken and dysfunctional home I grew up in. As I got older, I saw all my limitations connected to my abuse and brokenness. My insecurity, fear, inability to read, self-hatred, lack of trust, hurts, anger, and pain were all connected to my past abuse. I had a chip on my shoulder. I felt robbed of a childhood and upbringing. I was angry. I let that anger grow and allowed it to justify my belief that this world owed me something. People and counselors would say, "You have the right to be angry." I interpreted that to mean I had the right to have a poor attitude.

> *"In your anger do not sin": Do not let the sun go down while you are still angry, and do not give the devil a foothold.*
>
> *- Ephesians 4:26-27 NIV*

When I got corrected, failed at something, felt rejected, or dismissed, I never took responsibility or tried to find out why. I would just say, "It is not my fault. It is because of what happened to me." I would always blame it on the events of my past. Going through life and having a ready-made excuse may seem like a good plan in theory, but it is not. I will never forget the times I was challenged and called out by people who loved me and cared enough about me to address my attitude and my perspective. I was angry that they dared to challenge my excuse! I railed, "Don't take this from me!" I thought this excuse was all I had. It was a comfort to have my own personal get out of jail free card. They were loyal friends who saw my excuse for what it was, a crutch that would hinder, hurt, and cripple me. They dug in with patience, love, wisdom, and good teaching, and prayed for me. I had to humble myself and soberly look at my circumstances, decisions, and actions. I learned to recognize that my actions were not solely because of my past.

> *When pride comes, then comes disgrace, but with humility comes wisdom.*
>
> *- Proverbs 11:2 NIV*

I understand that my past is part of me, but it does not own my future. Slowly, and I mean s l o w l y, my mind and thoughts began to change. Although, when I felt I was pushed too hard, I would run back to my familiar excuse. It was my default, it was easy. I understood it, even though it was not right nor was it healthy for me. It was an easy lie to believe, but it was a lie and nothing good comes out of a lie. My flesh wanted the easy way out and my past kept calling. That lie was a chain connecting me to my abuser and giving my past control over my future, tethering me to my pain.

> *Then you will know the truth, and the truth will set you free."*
>
> *- John 8:32 NIV*

How do you destroy a lie? You tell the truth. I had to admit what I was doing, repent, and turn to God. I was challenged to not always blame my past. I had to trust God to change me and remember that I became a new creation when I accepted Christ into my heart. No longer could I say this happened because of my past. Now, I had to ask myself, "What can I learn from this?" No longer would I identify myself as broken and abused. Now, I identify myself as redeemed; I am a new creation.

> *Therefore, if anyone is in Christ, he is a new creation; old things have passed away; behold, all things have become new.*
>
> *- 2 Corinthians 5:17 NKJV*

Life was scary without my excuse. I had to learn to be genuine and true to myself. It was a tough, vulnerable place to be when all you know is pain. The Lord took me on a journey through prayer and His Word. It became a wonderful place to be because I did not just know pain anymore. I knew the love of God, the mercy of the cross, the strength of the Spirit, and the hope of faith. With that new perspective and through the truth, I knew I was not alone. No longer did I have a chip on my shoulder, now I have a rock to stand on.

Humble yourselves before the Lord, and he will lift you up.
- James 4:10 NIV

The trail marker of freedom gives us the wisdom to seek the Lord and to extend grace to others.

TRAIL MARKER 8: CONFIDENCE

Is my confidence in my brokenness and manipulation of others, or do I have a true confidence in the Lord and the promises of God?

> *But blessed is the one who trusts in the Lord, whose confidence is in him.*
>
> *- Jeremiah 17:7 NIV*

Confidence was a concept I never really understood. While I knew its definition and I knew what it looked like in others. Confidence, value, and dignity were some of the deepest things my abuser stripped from me and some of the hardest things to be restored. To feel proud but not prideful, self-assured but not arrogant was not something I was taught. Abuse had left me broken, full of apprehension, valueless, insecure, and inferior. These words shaped how I viewed myself. The perversion of touch, truth, and love I had experienced left me empty. As a child, I built a system enabling me to survive, but it was flawed, built out of the brokenness around me. I must be worthless because I was used and discarded. Others were more important and valuable.

But you, God, see the trouble of the afflicted; you consider their grief and take it in hand. The victims commit themselves to you; you are the helper of the fatherless.

- Psalm 10:14

We are taught by example to reason, understand, love, respect, value and cherish those around us. For those raised in brokenness and dysfunction the values taught fall short of providing quality materials with which to build a strong, secure life. As I tried to sift through what lay before me, I found the scars not only from the abuse but also the pain of the generations before me holding me fast. Where my confidence lacked and the broken pieces of my past surrounded me, God came into my life and provided people who loved me.

Sing praises to God and to his name! Sing loud praises to him who rides the clouds. His name is the Lord—rejoice in his presence! Father to the fatherless, defender of widows—this is God, whose dwelling is holy.

- Psalm 68:4-5

Confidence comes from God who loves us, who sent His Son to die for us. Through His Word, and through the example of those who cared for and befriended me I learned what confidence really is. God taught me to reason, understand, love, respect, value and cherish those around me. My confidence is not in my successes or failures. My confidence is in God which allows me to be secure enough to be myself, just the way God made me. I surrendered my past to God who promises hope and a future and learned to be vulnerable and open.

I prayed and asked God to build in me the confidence that comes from knowing and loving my Savior and standing on His Word. I learned to put aside the former ways of thinking and to reason as a new creation, no longer the old man with his old habits and thoughts. God took my brokenness, sifted through the rubble of my past, released the tension of my scars, and built a strong, secure life in Him.

> *I will praise thee; for I am fearfully and wonderfully made: marvelous are thy works; and that my soul knoweth right well.*
>
> *- Psalm 139:14 KJV*

One of my blogger friends put it this way. I want to encourage you to "Be Yourself."

There is something about you that this world needs. If it weren't so you wouldn't have been created. You would not exist. Purpose is attached to your life. You are not supposed to be anyone else BUT yourself. Your greatest journey will happen when you start being you, while allowing God to work through you. When you trust God and take Him at His Word, you will discover things about yourself you did not know were there. It is like being on a treasure hunt, and YOU are the treasure!

> *For God, who said, "Let light shine out of darkness," made his light shine in our hearts to give us the light of the knowledge of God's glory displayed in the face of Christ. But we have this treasure in jars of clay to show that this all-surpassing power is from God and not from us.*
>
> *- 2 Corinthians 4:6-7*

When you truly embrace the person God intended you to be, it becomes your responsibility to nurture and value what God created in you. It is through this acceptance you will discover how to walk in true happiness! Through that understanding I found confidence in the One who died for me, holds me up and shines through me.

I pray the confidence found in Christ will be a trail marker for you.

TRAIL MARKER 9: SUBMISSION

Do I still submit to my old ways, my past and my hurts? Or do I submit to God's will, His Words, and His ways?

> *Do not conform to the pattern of this world, but be transformed by the renewing of your mind. Then you will be able to test and approve what God's will is—his good, pleasing, and perfect will.*
>
> *- Romans 12:2 NIV*

> *Submit yourselves, then, to God. Resist the devil, and he will flee from you.*
>
> *- James 4:7 NIV*

Submission is a difficult concept full of preconceived ideas and assumptions. It is a term that has been twisted by those who hurt and abuse others. The thought of submission can be very scary for those that have been broken, abused, and forced to do something against their will. True submission is placing yourself under the umbrella of God's divine plan, knowing that God loves you, and that regardless of what happens you are willing to follow His Word, His heart, and His Son. It means committing your life to follow Jesus who gave everything, holding nothing back for you.

We usually define submission as giving up or letting go. As a child I did not have a choice. My submission was forced, using abuse, lies, pain, and torture. I had to do whatever the one with the power dictated. The word submission had become a trigger word, lighting off a powder keg of emotions, causing a visceral reaction. I would explode, "DO NOT TELL ME TO SUBMIT, OR SURRENDER!"

When I turned my life over to Christ, God began a new work in me. As I grew deeper in my faith and stronger in my walk with the Lord, this concept of submission challenged me. I would shake my hand to heaven, remembering the times I was forced to submit against my will. It left me with scars that I will have for the rest of my life. "God, how can you ask me to submit? To surrender? The only thing I knew about submission was demeaning and painful.

Before I was going to submit, I had to learn about what it truly meant. I had to learn the beauty and peace that comes from complete surrender and true submission to God. I chose to place myself under the umbrella of God's divine plan, knowing that God loved me, and that regardless of what happened, I was willing to follow His Word, His heart, and His Son; who gave everything, and held nothing back for me.

> *"Father, if you are willing, take this cup from me; yet not my will, but yours be done."*
>
> *- Luke 22:42*

> *"Abba, Father," he said, "everything is possible for you. Take this cup from me. Yet not what I will, but what you will."*
>
> *- Mark 14:36*

God will ask us to do many difficult things on our journey as we travel in our relationship with Him. Surrender unconditionally, submit wholeheartedly, pray unceasingly, worship faithfully, confess honestly, and forgive completely, to name just a few. These tasks are extremely difficult and beyond our ability apart from Christ. They take time. They require you to allow God's love and mercy to debride your wounds and wash over you with His cleansing power. You will need to trust the Lord's scalpel to dislodge, and remove hardened parts of your heart, and cancerous thought processes from your mind. Throughout this healing process, practice being still and quiet before the Lord, listen carefully and learn to distinguish His voice from the noise and chaos that so often surrounds us. Accept the softened heart, renewed mind, and new life the He provides for you.

> *Be still in the presence of the Lord, and wait patiently for him to act.*
>
> *- Psalm 37:7a NLT*

> *May God himself, the God of peace, sanctify you through and through. May your whole spirit, soul and body be kept blameless at the coming of our Lord Jesus Christ.*
>
> *- 1 Thessalonians 5:23*

Allow God to fill your heart, life, spirit, and soul; flooding out the impurities this world has filled you with. When God reveals the attitudes, fears, anger, lust, and lies you thought had been removed, give them to Him again and allow Him to wash you clean. There is no shame in cleaning up, life is messy.

> *Create in me a clean heart, O God; and renew a right spirit within me.*
>
> *- Psalm 51:10 KJV*

Know that God is for you not against you. Let the testimony of God's work in your life shine. Our God is alive. He is present and active in our lives regardless of how it looks to us.

> *And we know that in all things God works for the good of those who love him, who have been called according to his purpose.*
>
> *- Romans 8:28 NIV*

Submission is not so scary when you know that the one you are submitting to loves you extravagantly, unconditionally, and completely. It is no longer evil or dark because you know the one you're submitting to is full of goodness, light, hope, and grace. It is impossible to submit everything to God in a single day. Instead, I look back and realize my submission to God was incremental. Each day I spent in His presence led me to know Him more, and the more I knew Him, the more I was willing to give Him. Truly walking in His grace is a step-by-step, dying to self, journey. But living a life rich in God's gifts of love, mercy, and grace is worth every step.

> *And so, dear brothers and sisters, I plead with you to give your bodies to God because of all he has done for you. Let them be a living and holy sacrifice—the kind he will find acceptable. This is truly the way to worship him.*
>
> *- Romans 12:1 NLT*

I don't submit because I'm weak. I don't submit because I'm a fool. I submit because God loves me. He called me to be a living sacrifice. I can trust His Word and know that He is with me. Submission is where I learned to be strong. Like many of the trail markers, this one lead me to the One who created me for a purpose, who loved me before anyone saw me, and who would take the shattered remains of what the enemy meant for evil and use it for His glory, creating beauty and life out of ashes and destruction.

I pray the trail marker of submission will also guide you to the One who loves you and created you for a purpose.

TRAIL MARKER 10: FORGIVENESS

When I stand at the base of a mountain that I have prepared mentally and physically to climb, I am reminded that the journey will be full of both beauty and challenges. Taking a moment, I pause to talk to the Lord before taking the first step. Having packed the right equipment, I look for the trail marker to confirm I am embarking on the right path.

Somewhere along that hike you get your first glimpse of the summit. It is a moment every hiker appreciates and reflects on, realizing how far they have come but also knowing how far they still need to go. It is both humbling and exciting to realize what you've already accomplished while knowing there is still so much more ahead.

> *It is God who arms me with strength and keeps my way secure. He makes my feet like the feet of a deer; he causes me to stand on the heights.*
>
> *- Psalm 18:32-33 NIV*

Like a hiker that embarks on a journey, those who have accepted Christ also embark on a journey. The hiker's journey is one of adventure, with steep cliffs and deep valleys, breathtaking views, difficult terrain, and tests of endurance. Reaching the summit and sharing the adventure with others make the difficulties experienced along the way worth it. Likewise, the Christian's journey is a lifetime adventure with God, also filled with steep cliffs and deep valleys, breathtaking views, difficult terrain, and tests of endurance. Sharing the adventure with others and reaching heaven make the difficulties experienced along the way worth it.

> *"Go into all the world and preach the Good News to everyone."*
>
> *- Mark 16:15 NLT*

The first serious hike I took, my friend recommended I get hiking poles. I borrowed a pair, and at first, it was very awkward to walk with the hiking poles because I was not used to them. I was used to depending on myself. Slowly, I realized how much I needed them and depended on them. For days after that hike, I walked around looking for the hiking poles. I had used them to keep my balance, test the ground before me, and reassure myself that every step I took was safe. They had become an extension of myself. God's Word and the Holy Spirit are like those hiking poles, keeping me balanced, assessing the ground that I'm walking on, and aiding when the terrain is difficult.

On our journey, God lovingly reminds us how much He has forgiven us, and what He did on the cross to rescue, save, and redeem us from the price of sin. He has forgiven us our trespasses, our mess ups, our mistakes. Christ's forgiveness has given us everything. Forgiveness for me simply means freedom. Freedom from my sin. Freedom from my past. Freedom from my fears. Somewhere along the journey we get a glimpse of a higher calling. We come to a crest and recognize the depth of this journey is so much more. We have come so far and accomplished so much. We see for the first time, there is still so much more ahead, as the Lord asks us to forgive those who have trespassed, messed up, and sinned against us.

> *Be kind and compassionate to one another, forgiving each other, just as in Christ God forgave you.*
> *- Ephesians 4:32 NIV*

There are times when you need to evaluate the items brought on a hike, keeping only what is essential, because the added weight of unnecessary items will weigh you down. You need to be willing to part with them to lighten your load, making it easier to accomplish your goal of reaching the summit. There are times when God asks us to evaluate things in our life, thoughts, attitudes, habits, and possessions keeping only what is essential and beneficial. We can then walk forgiven and free from our burdens.

> *Give your burdens to the Lord, and he will take care of you. He will not permit the godly to slip and fall.*
> *- Psalm 55:22, NLT*

As we grow in our relationship with the Lord and experience His forgiveness; we realize that we are a reflection of what God has done in us. We are a living testimony for others to see God's love, grace, and forgiveness reflecting in us. This realization helps me forgive others who have hurt or rejected me, even those who abused me.

O Lord, you are so good, so ready to forgive, so full of unfailing love for all who ask for your help.

- Psalm 86:5 NLT

Forgiveness is not an easy mountain to climb. It takes sacrifice, persistence, and commitment. God has shown us how to forgive through the example of His Son. God so loved you, He gave His one and only Son. The sacrifice that the Son of God willingly made when He died on the cross provided forgiveness for all of us. The commitment He asks of us is not a commitment that we are able to make in our own ability. But He promises us that He will be with us always, giving us the strength and ability that we need. Through His strength we can persistently forgive as the waves and memories of the hurt, pain, and rejection threaten to overwhelm us again. We are never alone in these depths. He reminds us that He will never leave us, nor forsake us. When we are weak and struggling, He is strong. It is through His strength that we can successfully navigate the difficulties of our journey.

Give all your worries and cares to God, for he cares about you.

- 1 Peter 5:7 NLT

Today, I stand on the confession that by grace, I am saved by faith. I am no longer the broken 16-year-old kid who walked into a church and said a sinner's prayer, "Lord, come into my life, forgive me for my sins, become my Lord and Savior." This prayer has echoed throughout my life and has kept me grounded. Out of all the prayers I've prayed, I know that prayer on that day changed my life forever. Christ became my Lord and Savior. He became the Ruler of my life, the Guide, and Director of my steps. He is my Savior, the One who paid the ransom for me, made a way, took my guilt, my sin, and my shame.

I know I am a sinner saved by grace that needs the love of God. He died for my sins, forgave me, set me free, and made me new. I drank from the cup of His forgiveness, ate from His bread of life, and have been humbled by His love at the foot of the cross. The realization of the magnitude of what He did for me, and the promise of hope in my life helps me pour out forgiveness to others. This journey is an ongoing, lifelong adventure for all of us. There are days when we feel stronger, and days when we need to pray and ask God for the strength to keep going. Have I truly forgiven the pains of my past and let my selfishness and fleshly desires die? Have I let the freedom that God has for me through forgiveness become a reality?

> *Therefore, if anyone is in Christ, the new creation has come: The old has gone, the new is here! All this is from God, who reconciled us to himself through Christ and gave us the ministry of reconciliation:*
> *- 2 Corinthians 5:17-18 NIV*

I had to seek the Lord and challenge myself on the journey of forgiving the nightmare. When I got lost in my pain, I would look for the trail markers as the Lord shined His light, illuminating the right path. When I got filled up with pride, I would cry out to God and look for the markers as He steered me back to the path. When I got overwhelmed with memories of the past that seemed to scream louder than the hope of the future, I would hold tight to God as He guided my steps and pointed out the right trail markers. My hope is that these trail markers will help you stay on your path, forgive your nightmare, and overcome your past as you trust in the Lord.

Trust in the Lord with all your heart and lean not on your own understanding; in all your ways submit to him, and he will make your paths straight. Do not be wise in your own eyes; fear the Lord and shun evil. This will bring health to your body and nourishment to your bones.

- Proverbs 3:5-8 NKJV

PART III

| BREAKING OUT |

VICTIM TO VICTORIOUS

What a slogan, what a concept, what a title! For much of my life I saw myself as a victim, allowing the abuse to be my identity and allowing the words of others to guide me. Those words led to self-hatred. What are the steps, the actions that lead me from victim to victorious?

How To Break the Trap of Victimhood?

1. I started praying more earnestly. I called out to God with the belief that He was real, He was there, and He would do something in me.

2. I started to read the Bible, but more than just reading it, I started listening to it and doing my best to apply it to my life.

3. I had to be honest with myself, not every terrible thing that happened in my life was because of what I went through.

4. I had to evaluate myself soberly and honestly. I had to learn to change, to learn it was OK to change and be confident. I had to put into practice a healthy mindset and treat myself with value.

5. I had to repent from my expectation that this world owed me something.

6. I had to stop manipulating others and myself.

7. I had to learn to be content.

8. I had to learn that not everything was my fault.

9. I had to learn why I was trying to control others.

10. I had to learn why I was still trying to appease people for protection.

Many of these things are still a work in progress. I still have to lose myself in prayer, in the Word of God, and in worship. Yet, I truly learned to die to self — the old man — and live with a new hope. Not a hope I could conjure up, but the hope given to me on the cross of Calvary. How do I move from victim to victorious? I believe God's Word, I stay close to the Lord in prayer, and I worship him every day. The Lord brings me to a place of remembrance. I am no longer a victim. I am victorious.

Breaking the Trap of Victimhood

1. I started to pray:

> *You will seek me and find me when you seek me with all your heart.*
>
> *- Jeremiah 29:13 NIV*

As a young person I was taught, be good and you will go to heaven. I was not taught how to pray or how to seek the Lord. When I did pray, my prayers were always self-centered. I asked the Lord to bless me, protect me, give me... At its core, this is not a negative prayer at all. We all want protection and provision. However, God desires so much more for us.

> *Pray like this: Our Father in heaven, may your name be kept holy. May your Kingdom come soon. May your will be*

done on earth, as it is in heaven. Give us today the food we need, and forgive us our sins, as we have forgiven those who sin against us. And don't let us yield to temptation, but rescue us from the evil one.

- Matthew 6:9-13 NLT

And pray in the Spirit on all occasions with all kinds of prayers and requests. With this in mind, be alert and always keep on praying for all the Lord's people.

- Ephesians 6:18 NIV

What I mean when I say I started to pray, is I started to go beyond the bless me, protect me, and give me prayers and began to truly surrender to God's will and plan for my life. I desired the fullness of God, no longer on my terms, but His. I needed to let go of control and let God move in the way He wanted to move, trusting God would move in my life for His glory. Sometimes His moves were comfortable, other times they were challenging and humbling, but they always lined up with His Word. I started seeking God more and my needs less.

You, God, are my God, earnestly I seek you; I thirst for you, my whole being longs for you, in a dry and parched land where there is no water.

- Psalm 63:1 NIV

2. I started to read God's Word – the Bible

All Scripture is God-breathed and is useful for teaching, rebuking, correcting and training in righteousness,
- 2 Timothy 3:16 NIV

I remember our family Bible was big, but it was never opened except to put flowers in after a funeral. I remember exactly where it sat in our home, it even had a metal clasp to hold it closed. As a child, I was intimidated by it. The Bible was something holy, it was God stuff. The few times I saw it opened I recalled the artwork. I was very much in awe of the Bible, yet it seemed inaccessible to me and that lead me to believe it was not for somebody like me.

Years later, when somebody gave me a Bible and asked me to read it, the familiar feeling of intimidation came over me again. In the beginning when I started to read the Bible, it was not to learn. I was trying not to offend the Bible. It still seemed so far above me and inaccessible. While seeking to fit in at church I quickly learned that if I could quote the Bible, I would be celebrated and given praise. At first, I memorized scriptures for the praise I received, but God's Word is alive and active. It is His Word… for me!

> *As the rain and the snow come down from heaven, and do not return to it without watering the earth and making it bud and flourish, so that it yields seed for the sower and bread for the eater, so is my word that goes out from my mouth: It will not return to me empty, but will accomplish what I desire and achieve the purpose for which I sent it.*
> *- Isaiah 55:10-11 NIV*

Throughout my life, I've met many people who have used the Bible as a hammer just to prove a point, not to soften their heart. Finally, I started to read the Word of God to learn from it and grow from it, not simply to get something out of it. Instead, I read to get to know Him and grow in my relationship with Him. I started to change. God took my heart of stone and made it a heart of flesh. He transformed my mind helping me to understand His Word. I have truly tried to become a doer of God's Word not just a hearer of God's Word. God's Word is not for my gain but His glory.

> *I will give you a new heart and put a new spirit in you; I will remove from you your heart of stone and give you a heart of flesh. And I will put my Spirit in you and move you to follow my decrees and be careful to keep my laws.*
> *- Ezekiel 36:26-27 NIV*

> *Do not merely listen to the word, and so deceive yourselves. Do what it says.*
> *- James 1:22 NIV*

3. Not everything bad that happens in my life is because of what I went through.

> *"Come now, let us reason together," says the Lord: though your sins are like scarlet, they shall be as white as snow; though they are red like crimson, they shall be like wool."*
> *- Isaiah 1:18, NIV*

The unhealthy belief that every dreadful thing happens in my life because of what I went through, gave me an excuse and something to blame. Not every wrong or negative thing happened because of my past. Sometimes it was because of my big mouth, or because I was lazy or selfish. When the consequences of my actions caught up with me, it was always easier for me to say it was because I was abused.

The fact that I was abused is true and will never change. With that comes hurt and fears that I completely understand. I still wrestle with some today. Every time something triggers the hurts and fears I turn them over to God and He helps me through them.

One way I broke the trap of being a victim was to stop blaming everything on my abuse. Now I look at myself objectively and give myself freedom to inspect myself. I do not ignore my past, I simply learned not to blame my past for everything.

> *"Forget the former things; do not dwell on the past. See, I am doing a new thing! Now it springs up; do you not perceive it? I am making a way in the wilderness and streams in the wasteland.*
>
> — *Isaiah 43:18-19 NIV*

4. I had to learn to change, and learn it was OK to change. I had to put into practice healthy and honest things.

> *Finally, brothers and sisters, whatever is true, whatever is noble, whatever is right, whatever is pure, whatever is lovely, whatever is admirable—if anything is excellent or praiseworthy—think about such things.*
>
> — *Philippians 4:8 NIV*

Change is one of the hardest things to do, and practically impossible without God. When you are raised in a certain environment with expectations of unhealthy things, it is easy to see the world through the brokenness of your hurts. I learned as a child my value and my worth were insignificant. Through the process of breaking the mold of victimhood I had to learn it was OK to do healthy things and to seek honest things. I had to learn what healthy and honest things were. Where did I find that knowledge? In God's Word. I started to value relationships, education, dedication, commitment, and trust.

> *But the Holy Spirit produces this kind of fruit in our lives: love, joy, peace, patience, kindness, goodness, faithful-*

ness, gentleness, and self-control. There is no law against these things!

- Galatians 5:22 NIV

While I felt like those healthy things could never be a part of my life, I desired them. I no longer wanted to be shaped by the brokenness. I wanted to build on and look upon the good things of God. I put those things into practice, by not just being aware of them, but also practicing the healthy and honest things. First within myself, so I could display them to others.

I sought the Lord, and he answered me; he delivered me from all my fears. Those who look to him are radiant; their faces are never covered with shame. This poor man called, and the Lord heard him; he saved him out of all his troubles.

- Psalm 34:4-6 NIV

5. I had to repent from the expectation that this world owed me something. The Lord became my identity, not the abuse.

Restore to me the joy of your salvation and grant me a willing spirit, to sustain me.

- Psalm 51:12 NIV

I was cloaked in the pain and hurts of the past allowing the abuse to be my identity. I had to die to self and the unhealthy expectations I held on to because of the pain and hurt I went through. I felt like I was owed something to replace what was taken from me. This gave me an excuse for manipulation and justified my desires. Living with those expectations hurt the people who loved and supported me the most. It was wrong.

Past hurts do not determine my future. My past should not hold me back, therefore my past should not owe me anything. I had to repent not only for my actions but also for my attitude. I was wrong to think everyone owed me something. I came to understand and accept that God gave me everything I needed and allowed my identity to be in Him. I needed to celebrate what I had and not be angry or resentful for the things I did not.

> *You were taught, with regard to your former way of life, to put off your old self, which is being corrupted by its deceitful desires; to be made new in the attitude of your minds; and to put on the new self, created to be like God in true righteousness and holiness.*
>
> *- Ephesians 4:22-24 NIV*

My unhealthy expectations held me back because I felt God didn't want to set me free. My flesh had a chip on its shoulder, and a pain in its heart, but God made a way to freedom. His gift of repentance was given to me to break the chains of unhealthy expectations and manipulations. It was a light in a dark place like a word of encouragement in a time of need. I celebrated God's love, which surrounds me. I was reminded that Jesus died for me. His Word is here, given to encourage, comfort, and challenge me.

The Spirit of God still fills me, and my perspective has changed. I am no longer a broken child, but a child of God. My value is no longer shackled to my abuse. I am firm in my faith in Jesus, and I can walk in the promises He gave me.

> *For I am convinced that neither death nor life, neither angels nor demons, neither the present nor the future, nor any powers, neither height nor depth, nor anything else in all*

creation, will be able to separate us from the love of God
that is in Christ Jesus our Lord.
- *Romans 8:38-39 NIV*

The Lord helped me accept His forgiveness. I was a victim to the abuse, but I was also guilty of my own sin. One of my deepest wounds from the abuse was my shattered confidence. My self-worth and value were stolen. As a result, it was easier to believe everyone else deserves forgiveness. There was something inside me that taunted me and lied to me. It mocked that I didn't deserve forgiveness. I had forgiven others but struggled to receive forgiveness myself. I knew it was God's will for us to forgive one another and to walk in freedom. What you know, and what you do are often two different things. I knew what the Bible said about forgiveness, turning the other cheek, and praying for those who persecute you. I understood God loved me so much that He sent His son to die and pay the price of my sin. I read it, preached it, and truly tried to apply it, however, I never applied it to myself.

O Lord, you are so good, so ready to forgive, so full of
unfailing love for all who ask for your help.
- *Psalm 86:5 NLT*

I believe God desires to forgive me of my sins. It wasn't just about accepting the forgiveness. It was also about accepting the love and confidence that had been stolen. The confidence and love brought by the knowledge that I was accepted by God. In that confidence, through faith, I was able to accept God's forgiveness. I was then able to forgive myself for the mistakes and wrong things I had done. By the grace of God, I truly learned to forgive others who had sinned against me.

God showed me that self-care is not selfish care. Taking time to take care for yourself is not wrong or bad. Walking your journey with friends, family, counselors, coaches, and pastors is important and valuable. Going to your prayer closet, leaning on the Word, journaling, writing, and creating, are all part of the journey.

> *Where there is no guidance the people fall, But in an abundance of counselors there is victory.*
>
> *- Proverbs 11:14 NASB*

6. I had to stop manipulating others and myself.

> *For I am confident of this very thing, that He who began a good work among you will complete it by the day of Christ Jesus.*
>
> *- Philippians 1:6 NASB*

I define manipulation as trying to get other people to do what you want, and give you what you want, by any means possible. As an abuse victim I always had the trump card. My victimhood gave me the ability to win arguments and get the upper hand to gain what I wanted, mostly from the people I loved the most. That manipulation was simply wrong.

> *Set a guard over my mouth, Lord; keep watch over the door of my lips.*
>
> *- Psalm 141:3 NIV*

While trying to manipulate others, and believing that I was right for doing what I was doing, I ended up manipulating myself. I never let my own confidence or abilities speak for me, but always my identity was the abuse victim. The lie that I would never make it without my victimhood was so loud, I believed it. The lie behind the manipulation convinced me I was nothing but broken, useless, and empty. This was not what God saw in me. It was not what those who loved me saw either. While I hated that feeling of emptiness, it was so ingrained in me that I never felt my abilities held any value or importance. In the downward spiral of manipulation, you do what you hate because it is all that you know.

> *I do not understand what I do. For what I want to do I do not do, but what I hate I do.*
>
> *- Romans 7:15 NIV*

> *For we are God's handiwork, created in Christ Jesus to do good works, which God prepared in advance for us to do.*
> *- Ephesians 2:10 NIV*

God breaks the chains of manipulation through the power of His Word. He challenged the lies I believed and replaced them with truth. Truth that revealed the manipulation for what it was.

> *Therefore, if anyone is in Christ, he is a new creation; old things have passed away; behold, all things have become new.*
>
> *- 2 Corinthians 5:17 NKJV*

> *Do nothing out of selfish ambition or vain conceit. Rather, in humility value others above yourselves, not looking to your own interests but each of you to the interests of the others.*
>
> *- Philippians 2:3-4 NIV*

> *Do not let any unwholesome talk come out of your mouths, but only what is helpful for building others up according to their needs, that it may benefit those who listen. Be kind*

and compassionate to one another, forgiving each other, just as in Christ God forgave you.
- Ephesians 4:29, 32 NIV

The more time I spent with God and His Word, the more He transformed my thoughts. No longer did I see myself as broken, useless, and empty, but as a child of God.

May God himself, the God of peace, sanctify you through and through. May your whole spirit, soul and body be kept blameless at the coming of our Lord Jesus Christ. The one who calls you is faithful, and he will do it.
- 1 Thessalonians 5:23-24 NIV

Thanks be to God, who delivers me through Jesus Christ our Lord!
- Romans 7:25 NIV

The Lord taught me that anger is a part of life and how to manage it.

"In your anger do not sin": Do not let the sun go down while you are still angry, and do not give the devil a foothold.
- Ephesians 4:26-27 NIV

It (love) does not dishonor others, it is not self-seeking, it is not easily angered, it keeps no record of wrongs.
- 1 Corinthians 13:5 NIV

I brought my mind, heart, and life to Jesus and let God teach me and deliver me from the brokenness that lingered in my mind and spirit. I learned to accept who I am and what God has done in me. He is my rock.

> *I love you, Lord, my strength. The Lord is my rock, my fortress and my deliverer; my God is my rock, in whom I take refuge, my shield and the horn of my salvation, my stronghold.*
>
> *- Psalm 18:1-2 NIV*

7. I had to learn to be content.

> *You will keep in perfect peace those whose minds are steadfast, because they trust in you. Trust in the Lord forever, for the Lord, the Lord himself, is the Rock eternal.*
>
> *- Isaiah 26:3-4 NIV*

As an abuse victim, all I wanted to do was run away from my attacker, my problems, the dysfunction, and the pain. I was always looking beyond, past, and through, waiting for the next good thing. I was never happy in the moment because I was not content with what I had. I was wandering, always running, searching for more. Everything I have is in Christ: my joy, peace, strength, hope, and faith. Yet, in a flash I would still run. I had to learn to be content with little or with much. I had to stop running and realize it was OK. I was safe, and I could relax because everything I needed God had given me. He was teaching me, showing me, leading me, for His glory. He showed me how to stop and relax. No more running.

> *He says, "Be still, and know that I am God; I will be exalted among the nations, I will be exalted in the earth."*
> *The Lord Almighty is with us; the God of Jacob is our fortress.*
>
> *- Psalm 46:10-11 NIV*

While I knew everything I had wasn't perfect, it was good, complete, and true. Just like everyone else, my life has its ups and downs, joys and sorrows, but I have learned to be content with what the Lord has blessed me with. I don't run from life anymore. Now I run to Jesus.

> *I know what it is to be in need, and I know what it is to have plenty. I have learned the secret of being content in any and every situation, whether well fed or hungry, whether living in plenty or in want.*
> *- Philippians 4:12 NIV*

8. I had to learn that everything was not my fault.

> *But I say, walk by the Spirit, and you will not carry out the desire of the flesh.*
> *- Galatians 5:16 NIV*

Unfortunately, one of the common lies victims believe is that the abuse was their fault. Those who counsel us reassure us that it was not our fault. While we understand the truth with our mind, we still believe the lie in our heart. Believing the lie creates a heavy burden of anger and frustration.

> *I am exhausted from crying for help; my throat is parched. My eyes are swollen with weeping, waiting for my God to help me.*
> *- Psalm 69:3 NLT*

Sometimes we walk around desiring peace at any cost, even taking blame for things that were not our fault. Our desire for peace and calm can guide us to become a scapegoat, and we allow it because we desire peace at any cost. Other times we choose not to confront injurious behavior because it may shake the illusion of peace. Neither is healthy, good, or godly, but we do it anyway because of the desire for peace. Only God gives true peace.

> *The Lord is close to the brokenhearted; He rescues those whose spirits are crushed.*
>
> *- Psalm 34:18 NLT*

> *Do not be anxious about anything, but in every situation, by prayer and petition, with thanksgiving, present your requests to God. And the peace of God, which transcends all understanding, will guard your hearts and your minds in Christ Jesus.*
>
> *- Philippians 4:6-7 NIV*

> *Peace I leave with you; my peace I give you. I do not give to you as the world gives. Do not let your hearts be troubled and do not be afraid.*
>
> *- John 14:27 NIV*

One of the greatest steps towards breaking the bonds of victimhood was to realize that not everything was my fault. People do foolish things, regardless of whether I am around or not, and regardless of my past. Ignorance, foolishness, and selfishness are part of daily life, and I am not to blame for the actions of someone else. I was one of those who said sorry all the time, and most of the time I was apologizing for something that wasn't my fault. I just wanted peace. I had to learn that people get angry, but not always at me. I had to learn that when people get quiet, it doesn't always mean they're angry.

> *Grace, mercy and peace from God the Father and from Jesus Christ, the Father's Son, will be with us in truth and love.*
>
> *- 2 John 1:3 NIV*

9. I had to learn why I was trying to control others.

> *I weep with sorrow; encourage me by your word. Keep me from lying to myself; give me the privilege of knowing your instructions.*
>
> *- Psalm 119:28-29 NLT*

Why was I trying to control everyone? The simple answer – fear! If I was not in control, then I was afraid I would get hurt, betrayed, or abused again. I used my past to control others, but I was the one controlled by fear. I was consumed with fear of being a failure, of losing myself, and losing control.

> *I am losing all hope; I am paralyzed with fear. Let me hear of your unfailing love each morning, for I am trusting you. Show me where to walk, for I give myself to you. Teach me to do your will, for you are my God. May your gracious Spirit lead me forward on a firm footing.*
>
> *- Psalm 143:4,8,10 NLT*

Oh, I would tell myself lies and thought I knew better than most. I knew the right way. Why didn't people listen to me? Why didn't people do what I said? Didn't they understand? These are things I said to myself because truly, I wanted to be in control. I told myself I was looking out for others, but I was really trying to protect myself. For me, control was a shield to keep people at bay and my excuses justified me. I had to learn to let go and not be in control. I had to give the Lord control. He orders my steps. His Word is a light unto my path. May His will be done in my life. I cannot control anyone or anything.

> *The Lord makes firm the steps of the one who delights in him; though he may stumble, he will not fall, for the Lord upholds him with his hand.*
>
> *- Psalm 37:23-24 NIV*

> *Your word is a lamp to my feet and a light to my path.*
>
> *- Psalm 119:105 NKJV*

I humbly bring myself before the Lord. I no longer seek which way I should go, but I seek the Lord and He tells me which way to go. I still make plans for tomorrow, and I prepare for today, but I know the Lord is always with me. I have let go of control and given myself to God's will.

> *We can make our plans, but the Lord determines our steps.*
>
> *- Proverbs 16:9 NLT*

> *Trust in the Lord with all your heart and lean not on your own understanding; in all your ways submit to him, and he will direct your paths.*
>
> *- Proverbs 3:5-6 NIV*

Letting go and letting God has been amazing. While walking by faith can sound extremely exciting, it can feel very frightening, but I know God is always with me. When fear tries to overwhelm me and scream that I am not in control, I am gently reminded that I never was. But He is.

"The Lord himself goes before you and will be with you; he will never leave you nor forsake you. Do not be afraid; do not be discouraged."

- Deuteronomy 31:8 NIV

10. I had to learn why I was still trying to appease people for protection.

I have been crucified with Christ and I no longer live, but Christ lives in me. The life I now live in the body, I live by faith in the Son of God, who loved me and gave himself for me.

- Galatians 2:20 NIV

As children, we reason like a child and children expect to be protected, have security, love, and acceptance. But when abuse comes into a child's life they often feel alone, broken and a burden, so they build their own system of processes to protect themselves. The process I built was to be an appeaser. I thought being what everybody wanted me to be was safer. I would live whatever image somebody had of me and never show my real self.

I became a human chameleon. If somebody thought I was weak, I'd be weak. If they thought I was slow, I would be slow. If they thought I was broken, I would be broken. When you believe you are broken, you live broken. It was easy to let brokenness become my standard, my expectation, my identity. I remember arguing with myself and asking, what kind of value do I have? I would be whatever I thought people wanted because in hiding the real me I felt protected. I lost myself in the hiding, never revealing who I really was. I was lying to myself. I came to regret my role of chameleon. I came to hate it. But I did not know how to get out of it...until Jesus.

Turn to me and be gracious to me, for I am lonely and afflicted. Relieve the troubles of my heart and free me from my anguish.

- Psalm 25:16-17 NIV

Therefore if the Son makes you free, you shall be free indeed.

- John 8:36 NIV

I finally started to be myself. I almost didn't know what I stood for or what I believed. I was trapped as I tried to read the room. What did they want me to be? I never felt safe enough to be what God called me to be. Why would somebody want me? Why would somebody want to hear me? But Jesus…

When I am afraid, I put my trust in you. In God, whose word I praise— in God I trust and am not afraid. What can mere mortals do to me?

- Psalm 56:3-4 NIV

How did I discover where my confidence came from? I began to try to live what God called me to be. God showed me who I was as I sought Him. I found my strength, hope, and value in Him. He gave me my personality, gifts, and talents. I no longer wanted to try to blend in and be what I thought people expected me to be. Now I wanted to emulate Christ who died for me and set me free.

The Lord is my strength and my shield; my heart trusts in him, and he helps me. My heart leaps for joy, and with my song I praise him.

- Psalm 28:7 NIV

Be imitators of God, therefore, as dearly loved children and live a life of love, just as Christ loved us and gave himself up for us as a fragrant offering and sacrifice to God.

- Ephesians 5:1-2 NIV, 1995 ed.

GOING FORWARD

The journey of forgiving the nightmare continues in my heart, soul, and life. I am filled with many new revelations, a stronger faith, and a deeper love for my neighbor. I walk truly knowing the Lord is the lifter of my head.

> *But you, Lord, are a shield around me, my glory, the One who lifts my head high.*
>
> *- Psalm 3:3 NIV*

My testimony is not my identity. What I have been through has shaped me but does not own me. The sharing of my testimony is not to garner pity or for people to feel sorry for me, nor is it for profiting off my pain. The purpose of sharing my testimony is to help others on their journey to forgiveness.

My victories are in Jesus and my weaknesses are still before me. Life does not owe me anything because I was abused. The Lord taught me to forgive, and He set me free. He longs to lead you on your journey to forgiveness and freedom also. Every day the Lord is teaching me to be the man that He has called me to be: a father, husband, pastor, and friend. I am trusting the Lord to help me be that man. No matter what I do or where I come from, the Lord makes me who I am.

Learning to forgive does not mean life will be perfect, or that troubles and doubts will not come to my door. There will be challenges, victories, setbacks, and failures. There will be seasons of weeping and rejoicing. This is life. Jesus said:

> *"I have told you these things, so that in me you may have peace. In this world you will have trouble But take heart! I have overcome the world."*
>
> *- John 16:33 NIV*

Much of life is about attitude, and my attitude should be about the Lord. The fears, rejection, and abuse are what owned me, guided me, and lead me down roads littered with insecurities. As each fear, rejection, and trauma from the abuse was released to God, He changed my heart and renewed my mind. Now, I feel like a man with a new suit, a new garment. Shedding off the old thoughts, and putting on a new way of thinking, believing, and hoping. No longer does the rudder of unforgiveness steer my life. No more holding on to excuses or blaming myself or others. That pattern seemed so comfortable, familiar, and easy to do. Yet now I stand on the Word of God and put my trust in the Lord. The old is gone – the new has come!

> *Do not conform to the pattern of this world, but be transformed by the renewing of your mind. Then you will be able to test and approve what God's will is—his good, pleasing, and perfect will.*
>
> *- Romans 12:2 NIV*

Even though I don't know what tomorrow holds, I know who holds tomorrow. And the Lord will continue to lead me on this journey through its twists and turns and ups and downs. There is nothing that has happened or will happen that has taken, or will take, God by surprise. The Lord can and will use anything and everything in my life to bring Himself glory. My responsibility is to keep my eyes and my heart focused on Christ.

The way you feel about yourself is often the way you treat yourself, and how you let others treat you. In Christ we are loved, forgiven, and secure. In Christ we are adopted, justified, redeemed, reconciled, and chosen. In Christ we are victorious, filled with joy and peace. What a wonderful Savior is our Lord Jesus Christ!

It is challenging and a little overwhelming to be vulnerable, opening myself up to go where the Lord sends me and do what He tells me to do. I look forward to tomorrow, and believe I am ready for what is next, not because of my ability, but because of what the Lord has done in me. As I decrease, the Lord increases. May my testimony, my story, and my life always glorify the Lord. I pray that you will find the freedom I found in God's Word, the hope I found in faith in Christ, and the love I found in Jesus. I pray you too can forgive your nightmare.

ACKNOWLEDGMENTS

I would like to say thank you

To my wife and kids you keep me grounded in love and truth, our life of faith in Christ is an adventure.

To my sister (my second mom) even though you have walked through your own struggles, you have always been there for me. Your support and love is truly a gift.

To my brother, aunts and uncles, nieces and cousins thank you for all you have done.

To my friends and family who told me the truth even when I did not want to hear it, you supported me in the middle of the mess. On this journey grace abounds!!

To Mr Brown, who held up my hands and supported me as we wrote this book.

To Tim Twigg and the team at Arrow Press Publishing for all your help working with my wife and I in bringing this book that God laid on my heart to life.

To my illustrator Sonya Conners for all the time, effort, and hard work you put into the artwork for Forgiving the Nightmare Ministry.

To the churches who have prayed for me, I love you guys for being on my side, in my corner, a part of the team.

To those who read this book. As you read, please know what God has done for me, the Lord can do for you also.

To my Lord and Savior Jesus Christ, for Your grace that saves me, Your Word that fills me and Your love that surrounds me.

CONTACT

For more information about Mark, how to book him for a speaking engagement, or to share your story of forgiveness, visit:

WEBSITE:
https://www.forgivingthenightmare.com/

FACEBOOK:
https://www.facebook.com/forgivingthenightmare

CPSIA information can be obtained
at www.ICGtesting.com
Printed in the USA
FSHW012352091221
86819FS